"When I considered workplace engagement, [actions] a company takes to engage its worke[rs.] Inspired Work has turned my thinking upside down. In his signature program and book, *The Workplace Engagement Solution*, Harder postulates that yes, a company needs to offer a compelling mission and values. But each worker is responsible for her own personal mission, his unwavering commitment, their ability to fashion support systems. It's a 1/4 to 3/4 proposition, with 3/4 of the responsibility falling on the shoulders of the employee. After an initial gulp, I thought to myself, 'Wow, how wonderfully clear this take on workplace engagement is! And how richly empowering to call on a few simple tools to assume full responsibility for how we show up at work, every day!'"

—Achim Nowak, president of Influens, author of *The Moment*, TedX speaker

"As publisher and executive editor of a dominant, global business digest, I've had the opportunity to review over 14,000 essays over the years, covering the entire business spectrum. Rarely do I come upon the level of truly authentic, cutting edge thought leadership as discovered within *The Workplace Engagement Solution*. This isn't just a collection of anecdotal musings or rehashed wisdom, as espoused by the current plethora of leadership consultants hawking their latest revelations. What David has expertly crafted and delivered here is a rare and priceless commodity these days—candid, actionable insights based on years of 'in the trenches' experience. In doing so, he dares to question timeworn, conventional thinking and theory in a refreshingly disruptive manner. For any forward-looking professional at any level of any organization seeking to truly 'break the mold' with intentional engagement, this is the Book (and indeed, the Bible) for you."

—Dennis J. Pitocco, editor-in-chief, bizcatalyst360.com

THE
WORKPLACE ENGAGEMENT SOLUTION

Find a Common Mission, Vision, and Purpose
With All of Today's Employees

David Harder

CAREER
PRESS
Wayne, NJ

THE WORKPLACE ENGAGEMENT SOLUTION
Edited by Mary Campbell, PhD
Typeset by Diana Ghazzawi
Cover design by Ty Nowicki
Figure illustrations on cover by bloomua/depositphotos
Printed in the U.S.A.

To order this title, please call toll-free 1-800-CAREER-1 (NJ and Canada: 201-848-0310) to order using VISA or MasterCard, or for further information on books from Career Press.

The Career Press, Inc.
12 Parish Drive
Wayne, NJ 07470
www.careerpress.com

Library of Congress Cataloging-in-Publication Data

CIP Data Available Upon Request.

Dedicated to Patricia Wisne.

Your soul and your heart live on through everyone you touched.

Acknowledgments

Lisa Hagan, you are the proof that a literary agent can be brilliant and loving; Linda Sivertsen, my "book whisperer," you pushed and cheered me into becoming a very real writer; Paul Archambault, you lighten and brighten my every day; David Philp, your elegant mentorship has opened doors into a better life; Kim Shepherd, force of nature, you make full living my only alternative; Laura Garrett, my sister, friend, and confidante; Mindy Zasloff, house mother, brilliant talent expert, and colleague-for-life, Barbara Chardavoyne, every day you demonstrate love, kindness, respect, and care; Brenda Eddy, my mentor, wise elder, and friend, I am a better human being because of you; Larry Schwartz, an ideal example of all that can come out of this work, brilliant, kind, a role model and friend; Carolyn Soper, you elevate life to art and devote every day to skipping; Michael Beckwith, my spiritual inspiration; Safire Rose, who helped me dismantle anger and righteousness, and flood that void with light; Cherie Carter-Scott, who gave me the courage to jump without a parachute; and Gail Lapins, fearlessness personified, you gave me the foundation to pursue all that I want.

Contents

1

The Great Disengagement

According to Gallup's most recent global engagement survey, only 13 percent of the world's workers are engaged.[1] With numbers like this, how do we get anything done? Well, we do it in a trance.

The truth is that most of us want to be enthused, awake, involved, interested, happy, grateful, and connected with our work. We also want to work in environments that inspire these characteristics. But unfortunately, until we understand how our workers fell into "the trance" and learn how to end it permanently, billions will be needlessly lost in productivity and profit every single day.

This 13-percent work engagement statistic isn't a business problem; it is a national tragedy that extends far beyond the workplace. The malaise behind these figures impacts every aspect of our culture. The trance kills customer relationships, livelihoods, and personal satisfaction. The trance kills people. The trance shows up in the lab worker who lost the blood work or the receptionist who doesn't remember your name. The trance shows up in a doctor who mindlessly issues orders to everyone around him as you lay right there in his presence, fighting for your life. He never talks directly to you. I call it the great disengagement.

We encounter the great disengagement every single day. We run into it at the grocery store where someone tersely answers, "If it isn't on the shelf, we don't have it" or having products break just days if not hours after bringing them home. We recognize disengagement when our boss tells us to shut up or he'll make sure we regret it. We see it in the CEOs who blindly clip away at the bench strength of their organizations for lazy short-term financial gains. We feel it when flight attendants raise the temperature in the cabin of our plane, just so more passengers will sleep through their flights.

If 87 percent of the world is disengaged, the odds are high that we will only meet one person out of 10 who impacts us like an unexpected gift, a singular light that brightens our day. They may look us in the eye and tell us we are valued. We will remember them for sure. That is, unless we are also in a trance. And like an irritating and unwelcome friend, the trance follows us home to disengage our families. We pass the trance on to our children.

Attempts to break the trance have turned into a big business. Employee engagement is the single most popular talent initiative in organizations today. As Josh Bersin states, "CEOs are bending over backwards to make their company a 'great place to work.' Free food, unlimited vacation, yoga classes, and lavish educational benefits are becoming common. But as all this attention shifts toward the health and happiness of staff, employee engagement remains surprisingly low." Bersin cites Gallup, Glassdoor, and Quantum Workplace research; Gallup states one-third of employees are engaged, Glassdoor averages engagement at a C+ (3.1 out of 5), and Quantum Workplace says engagement is at its lowest level in about a decade.[2]

It takes just a bit of common sense to define why typical engagement initiatives produce single digit improvements or fail altogether. You will probably recognize the pattern:

1. The CEO or business owner realizes that disengagement is impacting profits and customer satisfaction. He or she walks down the hall to human resources and tells them to fix the problem.

2. The human resources executive launches an employee engagement initiative, but the employees look past his or her shoulder to the CEO for cues and they see "business as usual" or no real commitment.

3. An employee survey is issued. Quite often, employees feel patronized by questions that seem to really be asking, "How can you do more for us?"

4. The feedback is summarized and shared, usually succeeding in making managers feel even more inadequate to solve the problem.

5. We send the managers to a retreat center to become better leaders. They return more "enlightened" to employees who respond, "So what?"

The Workplace Engagement Solution doesn't mimic this old "top down" approach. What it does is offer a democratic process in which everyone is responsible, everyone participates, and everyone awakens. In my experiences creating engagement within organizations, it has become clear that when we build a great relationship with our work, not only does the organization improve, everyone's life gets better. Everybody wins.

For most of us, work is the biggest relationship that we have. Why a relationship? When we launched Inspired Work, my work engagement company, the practice of using career assessments was quite popular. But an assessment only measures superficial aspects and truths about a person's skills and probable best roles. A great relationship towards work, on the other hand, requires a wide variety of characteristics that include the person's outlook, gifts, beliefs, life skills, and behaviors. Each characteristic influences the other. For example, someone can be on the right path but failing because they are missing the necessary life skills to be successful. Without knowing what those life skills are, the individual may define their career as a failure. But when we discover that those missing life skills are learnable, we immediately have access to the tools for building a highly successful relationship with work. And, we consistently find deep and meaningful value when a person explores each characteristic of their relationship with work versus relying on the limited views of assessments, surveys, and performance reviews.

During the last 25 years, I have helped more than 42,000 professionals transform their relationship with their work. Thousands of them have launched new careers. Thousands have become business owners for the first time. Even more have become far more effective and happier in their existing careers. For many years, we used the program for individual applications and eventually created separate leadership and learning programs for whole organizations. There was some concern that if we got employees to define what they wanted out of life and how to get it, they would leave, but that changed when we began giving the program to intact teams. Instead of leaving, employees experienced an opening up of their minds and hearts to elevate their entire experience of work together. They committed to each other. Employee engagement figures soared, and by introducing a few simple internal rituals, the breakthroughs were not only sustained, they expanded over time.

The bottom line is that we all spend most of our waking hours driving to, being at, coming home from, and recovering from work. When individuals consciously navigate their way into a great relationship with their work, not only does life improve, they become highly engaged and satisfied.

From all of these watershed experiences, I am going to share how to "crack the code" of employee engagement and build cultures that are energized, enthused, fluid, and capable of not only absorbing enormous change, but actually exploiting change to everyone's benefit. The investment is worthwhile because not only will profit and performance improve, but you will also serve to build tomorrow's workforce. *The Workplace Engagement Solution* isn't an advertisement for another big consulting contract. In fact, all that is required is an internal orientation, a dose of courage, a "book club," and an organizational change of heart.

It has become clear that full employee engagement is elusive due to two critical missing pieces:

- **Engagement only works as a democratic process.** It is futile to expect an awakening when we use the old hierarchical model of pushing leaders to become skilled at drawing engagement out of talent. They will not respond to more manipulation. They need and crave personal involvement and individual transformation.

An awakened organization requires that everyone is involved. In a democracy, everyone is responsible for the end result. It is a mistake to assume that the leaders are more engaged than the rest of the population. Indeed, I have met line workers who are more engaged than some of the leaders in charge of engagement programs. We all have much to learn from anyone, no matter the level, who shines in the area of self-driven change and engagement with their work.

In a true democracy, everyone is responsible in the process of learning how to change and engage. The leaders and managers can provide the right conditions, but they are not ultimately responsible.

- **We need to provide people with the skills to break out of the trance.** For years, academics, management consultants, and human resource professionals have discussed the "broken employment contract." But, as we lost the promises and assurances of the Industrial Revolution, organizations have typically failed in defining what it is that we need to do in order to thrive within the rapid, disruptive, and transformative change we find ourselves in. By extension, much of today's talent has obsolete work skills and no new life skills. Consequently, they become overwhelmed in simply trying to keep up with change. We need to help them close these gaps.

In 1970, the great futurist Alvin Toffler predicted that technology would accelerate the rate of change to such dizzying levels that by the turn of the century, most people would be in a perpetual state of shock trying to absorb too much change in too short a period of time. This "future shock" directly ties into the going-through-the-motions behavior that typifies today's trancelike, disengaged worker.[3]

We are emerging from a 300-year cycle called the Industrial Revolution. During this cycle, we were conditioned to view change as threatening, dangerous, and unsettling. Yet, thriving today requires more than just coping with change. The wisest of us are not only developing the skills for self-change, they are establishing an enthusiasm for growth, because growth is the new game and it offers far greater payoffs than the era of survival and predictability.

How many of us are conscious enough to be excited about trading in a sense of security for perpetual growth? Most of us need to be educated to even realize what the opportunity means on a personal level. For the vast majority, real change is a frightening prospect. For example, when we began our programs in 1990, most of our participants were pursuing one big professional change. After making that transition, many would tell me, "I'm glad that is over." But it wasn't over. The world just became faster and faster until now, when many people are too confused to even define what it is that they want. Now, imagine how much the national workplace will improve if we develop a thirst for learning and growth within ourselves and throughout our organizations.

It will require us to reinvent, learn, unlearn, and relearn in shorter periods of time. When we ask or order our employees to "snap out of it" or "get used to it," how can most of them comprehend how to do that? Yet many leaders continue to display the "do it or else" tactic in a world in which talent pools are filled with experts in going through the motions. Similarly, this idea that people should somehow be skilled at continuous personal change is equally far-fetched. This is why organizations, realistically, must develop their workers to not only understand change, but to learn how to change themselves continuously.

But let's get real. There isn't a corporate budget in the world to pay for the consulting fees it would take to do this. Yet, when we move the entire process in-house where it belongs, the financial investments are minimal, especially when we factor in the increases in performance and engagement that will ensue. This is much more an investment in time and energy. It is also, simply, what it will take to get beyond these real challenges we are facing.

As we proceed, we will examine why so many workers are still ensnared by the cataclysmic breakdown of the old industrial-based work paradigm and why it is good business to invest in their future. Developing a change program for these individuals is far more valuable than showing them the door and trying to recruit from the small slice of available talent out there that has already mastered the game of engagement.

There is also good news. Personal change is learnable. In *The Workplace Engagement Solution*, it is equally important to develop the skills of unlearning and identifying beliefs and behaviors that no longer serve us, no matter how we might desire to cling to the past. Consequently, skilled self-inquiry represents a vital beginning to this process.

In a world in which many media and political messages pine for the past, we need to be posting a new message: **Change is everyone's responsibility.** In front of us is a world filled with more opportunity to craft successful lives than ever before. But in order to fulfill that opportunity, we have to learn how to change on very personal and fundamental levels. We need to embrace continuous education and self-inquiry. Why? Because without a compelling and personalized sense of mission, vision, and purpose to fuel internal motivation, employees will lack the initiative, the "juice," to go through the challenges inherent in actualizing the personal change that is required.

Welcome to the reality of future shock. During the last 30 years, we progressively removed predictability and survival from the workplace. Then, technology introduced change with such growing ferocity that today's average college graduate will change careers, not just jobs, an average of four to six times. If we dare to expect the majority of our workers to engage, we need to help them become change experts in ways that are not only valuable for our organization, but personally meaningful as well. Like every other set of skills, when and if our capacity to personally change becomes as natural as other relevant skills—navigating software platforms, mastering social media advertising, and the like—we will become more effective in responding to other organizational, market, and technical changes that are continuously coming at us.

Is this outcome attainable? Absolutely.

I have both inspired and witnessed the human capacity to change and transform more than 40,000 times. These experiences have made me both an optimist and a realist—perhaps not a bad combination as we move forward. So let's get on with it.

We begin with the state of the CEO or business owner. If 87 percent of the world's talent is disengaged, the probability of CEOs also being actively disengaged is pretty high. With a purely democratic solution, the global disengagement problem can only be solved if everyone from the entry-level worker to the CEO/owner is dealing directly with his or her own engagement.

Engaged CEOs lead their cultures. The very word "engagement" implies connectedness and transparency. As I have already pointed out, the failure of most engagement programs begins when the CEO turns the initiative over to someone else. Make no mistake about it, engagement includes an emotional component, and many CEOs are uncomfortable with the feelings generated by the human side of business. Others are so absorbed in dealing with market and shareholder expectations that they believe they cannot add culture concerns to their crowded plates. Nothing could be more wrongheaded.

It might still seem counterintuitive for CEOs to feel they should be saddled with culture development, but developing awakened cultures is what makes the job of the CEO much easier. In fact, as I coach and consult with many chief human resources officers while they navigate themselves into new careers, I always ask the question, "Is the CEO leading the culture?" If the answer is no, I tell the client to "keep their bags packed." I also tell them that it will not be worthwhile to do an engagement program because regardless of the circumstances, the results will be the same: mediocrity or outright failure. Bottom line? Wasted time, effort, and dollars.

This challenge becomes even clearer when we accept that engagement and personal change are challenging for all of us. The journey from disengagement to engagement requires deep personal change and some new life skills. Unfortunately, too many of us still fear the predictable discomfort of personal change and avoid it at all costs. We do not even understand that we are working against our own best interests. We lack the insight. We don't know what we don't know.

Therefore, it is critically important for the CEO or business owner to "wise up" to this cause-and-effect relationship within a culture. She or he needs to become the first to put their feet to the fire and embrace the life-altering possibility of becoming a deep personal-change role model. Now this is something to get excited about.

Indeed, we consistently find CEOs of category leaders such as Tesla, Apple, HBO, and Google who live and breathe this commitment. But before we start discussing category leadership, we must understand why fully awakened employees are so hard to find. Perhaps the greatest psychic leap that is in front of us is to move beyond the fixation on equating security with the routine. If we do this, and if we help others to do the same, the great opportunity is to develop lives and cultures filled with an enthusiasm for growth. But getting started requires that we get beneath the surface to understand why there is so much cynicism, contempt, aimlessness, and resignation around the topic of work. In other words, "How the bleep did we get here?"

For a full answer we need to go back in time. The Industrial Revolution has had an iron grip on our culture for the past three centuries. Clearly this era was over by the end of the 20th century. Even Y2K now seems like distant and quaint memory. The changes in front of us collide with the beliefs about work that our parents, grandparents, and many employers offered up as absolute truths. And though most of us understand this, few of us know how to move beyond these beliefs to become more effective participants in a modern landscape filled with whole new ways of living and working.

Prior to the dawn of the Industrial Revolution, change took place at a far more glacial pace. People spent most of their time and money growing or buying food. Making even one garment by hand took days. Industry resided in cottages. Child mortality was so high that many people had large numbers of children hoping that one or two would survive. Education was reserved for landowners, nobility, and the religious elite. The rich and powerful did not pay taxes while poor people paid rent *and* taxes.

The first great turning point in the world of work took place almost three hundred years ago. At that time, the British called the shots for how the rest of our world functioned. It was the most studied country on the face of the earth. In 1733, an English watchmaker named John Kay invented a simple machine called the Flying Shuttle. Its purpose was to improve the productivity of weaving. One person was now able to do the work of three. Fueled by riches, this innovation tipping point quickly turned into a tidal wave. Water and steam power moved the textile industry into high gear. The first inexpensive process for the mass production of steel was invented. We moved from scarcity of food to storehouses of abundant supply. Now producing more goods than any other country, England needed to find ways to get these products to other countries. Roads were built and boats got steam engines. Rails were laid. Landowners became industrialists. The banking industry was invented to grease the skids and the UK developed a world of consumers.

The Industrial Revolution represented an intoxicating leap forward in the evolution of civilization. The architecture behind this revolution introduced goods and services that were previously available to only the wealthy. In a parallel to today's work landscape, the Industrial Revolution resulted in the handing out of pink slips to virtually every worker from the previous era, but work didn't go away, it simply changed. This phenomenon is also taking place today. As old structures and dynamics go away, we need to become more fluent in seeing where new structures and dynamics emerge, because emerge, they always do. The difference? Three hundred years ago, it often took decades to change. Today, it can happen in a matter of days.

The old revolution also developed an unquenchable thirst for workers. Industrialists developed a recruitment pitch filled with standards and beliefs that haunt us today:

"If you come to work for us, we will give you survival and predictability."

To most of those working on farms, hunting for food, or dealing with the day-to-day uncertainty of keeping that cobbler shop in business, the pitch sounded really good. Human capital nourished the machine, which took center stage in our work. Parents, schools, organized religion, and governments prepared a new labor force that fit into the assembly lines, plugging bolts into holes. A new economy grew based on making large quantities of stuff. This worked for several hundred years. And, as with all personal or cultural advancements, there was also a price.

Predictability and survival didn't just become two in a series of standards. They became *the* standard. Although these standards made perfect sense at the time, consider how outdated they are now within our modern times. The fixation on predictability and survival dismisses joy, creativity, passion, engagement, full living, and connectedness to others. It often keeps us from new learning. Most profoundly, the old standards obscure the birthright of every man, woman, and child, which is to find and pursue what we were born to do. The growing awareness of this is also one of the seeds fueling today's discord with work. But, there was another great price we paid.

In *Critical Path,* Buckminster Fuller quantified predictions he had been making since the mid-1930s.[4] He warned the world that if we did not find ways to either eliminate or remove the poisons generated from fossil fuels and chemicals, the world would become uninhabitable by the turn of the century. Mr. Fuller must have died with a great deal of frustration because very few people listened to him. Most did not think about these issues because repetition produces a trancelike state. Fitting in, tending to our workstations, going through the routine became the mass trance of the Industrial Revolution. Most were happy for progress. Wages were small. Long hours were filled with back-breaking and repetitive work. Safety standards were appalling. In many factories, children were sent in to tend machines because the spaces were so small. If someone was injured or killed, others were waiting in line to step in and replace them. In fact, some of the laws passed during the early days of the Industrial Revolution indicate just how barbaric many employers were during that era. For example, the Factory Act of 1819 limited the work of children to 12 hours a day. And in 1833, children under the age of 9 were banned from working in the textile industry and 10- to 13-year-olds were limited to a 48-hour workweek.

Ironically, England's innovation also led to it losing its grip on the world. In the early days of the revolution, British leadership did its best to protect the country's manufacturing technology. But that progress opened up channels to the rest of the world. As mass production spread throughout the globe, other countries not only became more powerful, they turned into competitors. It wasn't long before every developed nation was playing the same game. And for the next 250 years, the Industrial Revolution dictated how we lived, consumed, worked, competed, and got educated. As the promise of predictability and survival evolved, we added various employee benefits: vacation plans, a retirement plan for when we grew old, medical coverage if we got sick, and so on. The most talented embraced it all and worked their way up the proverbial "career ladder."

On the shadow side, our ability to build stuff also fueled the bloodiest wars in the history of humankind. We leveraged wars with new technology and powerful capability to snuff life out in dramatic fashion. This led to the most awesome victories, but at a terrible price. But as we returned from world wars, manufacturing supremacy led to jobs for life, a comfortable middle-class living, and what was, for many, a comfortable routine. We worked, we saved, and we retired. The Industrial Revolution had successfully disrupted and transformed a culture that had stayed relatively the same for thousands of prior years.

In 1943, England dropped its next disruptive bomb on the world of work. A British engineer named Tommy Flowers demonstrated the first programmable computer to a stunned, skeptical room of military leaders. He developed this machine to decrypt German military code. It worked amazingly well. Ten of these "Colossi" were completed and used to gather intelligence. On June 5, 1944, a courier handed Eisenhower a note summarizing a Colossus decrypt. It confirmed that Hitler wanted no additional troops moved to Normandy. Moments later, he announced, "We go in tomorrow." The rest is history. The first computer may have actually played a bigger role in ending World War II than the first atomic bomb.[5]

Surprisingly, British leaders had the Colossi dismantled after the war. But, word of its power had gotten out. By 1946, the Eniac was invented and completed by J. Presper Eckert and John Mauchly at the University of Pennsylvania. The world's first digital computer occupied 1,800 square feet, used about 18,000 vacuum tubes, weighed almost 50 tons, and had less than half the power of a smart phone.

Whereas our first work revolution took hundreds of years, a new one was quietly birthed that day. This innovation would take just 50 years to completely change the way we live, work, think, learn, grow, and transform. The original wave from this technology would grow in ferocity and depth, disrupting virtually every work model we had developed over 300 years. In the mid-1990s, the wave made landfall and started to wipe out all of the promises and ideals of the industrial workplace.

Wouldn't it be great if the average human could change their behavior just as quickly? But, let us not get ahead of ourselves quite yet. The 1980s and early 1990s introduced two more revolutions that torpedoed once and for all the promise of predictability and survival. Financial deregulation quickly put the money people in charge of organizations. As companies lost the balance provided by marketing, human resources, and operations, jobs for life were replaced with dispassionate workforce planning sessions. People were moved and dismissed like, well, numbers. Insecurity replaced predictability and survival as our workers developed unprecedented levels of cynicism and contempt.

Profoundly, most workers craved a return to predictability and survival—to no avail, as this quest worked directly against the growing need to change, reinvent, and transform. Workers that thrived during this upheaval demonstrated high degrees of creativity and adaptability, qualities in short supply 20 to 30 years ago, if not still today. The rest hung on for dear life, hoping the human resources "death angel" wasn't coming around the corner. Unfortunately, these changes in our economic structure dictated that the angel would be making regular and more dramatic visits.

In 1976, two famed economists, Michael Jensen and William Meckling, published the now-legendary paper, "Theory of the Firm: Managerial Behavior, Agency Costs, and Ownership Structure."[6] In it, they argue that corporations needed to align the interests of management and shareholders. This new model changed how the corporate world conducts its business. For corporate executives, stock-based compensation became the alignment mechanism of choice. Consequently, their incomes skyrocketed. In the 1970s, CEOs of large, publicly traded companies earned less than $1 million in today's dollars. Today, that average has grown to $11.4 million. The new model motivates CEOs to focus incessantly on stock value over enhancing the real, longer-term performance of the company.

Also during the past 30 years, the entire investment market shifted from long-term investment in building organizations and markets to getting as much out of stock value in as short a period of time as possible. Investment banking turned into a multi-trillion-dollar industry. CEOs and hedge fund leaders became the foundation for how we dealt with workers in large organizations. With stock value becoming the number-one pursuit, American businesses and CEOs traded the long view for volatility, thus shifting the dynamic interests between capital and labor. As providers of capital push CEOs for greater and greater returns, cutting back on labor is the easiest way to signal they are addressing corporate financial performance.

Many workers are quite supportive of the American dream. But during the last 30 years, the average income has stagnated while hourly compensation has dropped. Workers witness venture capitalists taking advantage of financial deregulation to buy companies, take out loans on the assets, and pay huge dividends to themselves. Many of these acquisitions went bankrupt as employees lost their jobs, health insurance, and pensions. These financial barons are often celebrated and admired, but it has also resulted in mass income inequality at an alarming trend.

America's workers have watched their job and financial security go up in smoke. Anger, contempt, and cynicism turned into a raging fire as they read stories of greedy CEOs backdating stock options and pushing the envelope to unethical, and sometimes illegal, degrees. But perhaps it was amorality that angered them the most. In many organizations, the underlying message was that when needed, workers mattered. However, the cycles of hiring and laying people off reached such dizzying heights that we now have a labor force that basically understands that work has become more of a temporary assignment.

In 1990, I found a stronger path to self-realization. At the time, I was a successful executive in the staffing industry. I represented many of the largest film studios, six of the top-10 ad agencies, the Getty Trust, and many others. In economically good times, I was a headhunter with a team. During recessions, I moved over to supporting temporary labor solutions. Early that year, I remember a young woman coming into my office and saying, "You are so successful. How do you do it?" I responded, "In a coma."

At the time, it wasn't a particularly shocking admission. It was funny. I said it for laughs. At the heart of that terrible statement, however, existed the belief that most people didn't find joy, fulfillment, meaning, purpose, and success from work. For most of us, work was just a job.

Besides, the staffing industry wasn't what I really wanted to do with my life. As a respected jazz pianist and composer, what I wanted was a recording contract. In 1990, I received a call from a well-known jazz producer. He had inherited a truckload of money and was launching a new label within Warner Brothers Records. Six weeks into our project, he dropped dead of a heart attack.

For many of us, any brush with mortality is immediately followed by the timeless question *"What is the meaning of life?"*

After that terrible experience, it dawned on me that the only meaning I would ever find would be the meaning I, alone, could bring to my life. My producer's sudden passing brought home the fact that I was always putting happiness off to somewhere down the road and into the future. I knew little of value in how to be happy in the present, on a day-to-day basis. As I explored how to improve my life, it became clear that my entire relationship towards work would have to change. The enormity of that relationship became vividly important because work, for most of us, occupies most of our waking hours.

September 15 and 16, 1990 represented the dawn of my professional life as CEO of Inspired Work. I walked into a hotel ballroom and delivered the Inspired Work Program for the first time to 36 participants. The program has the magic of getting people to break with their past and design an ideal relationship with their work. For two days, I watched these remarkable souls dive into the process and emerge with dramatic shifts and new visions. I watched some of them walk in the door with a deep justification for their pain, only to loosen the grip of that pain because a new and personalized vision pulled them forward. I related personally to everything happening with the participants because it was also happening to me. In that first program, all of us found at least the beginnings of the lives we were meant to have. It also became clear to me that once we truly *experience* the truth, there is no going back.

A number of brilliant behavioral scientists and academics contributed to the model for that program, which forms a foundation for all the services we deliver today. We have now led thousands of individuals to use their own values to design a great relationship with their work. And for every participant, the definition of that relationship is unique.

About a year after we launched Inspired Work, one of the nation's largest banks became a client. After decades of success and stability, the CEO was looking for ways to generate more value for the shareholders. The plan backfired. During the next five years, waves of employees were laid off as the bank struggled to survive. They offered outplacement for those who wanted in finding another job, and they offered Inspired Work to those who wanted a new life. It was an amazing experience because they were individuals who came from the old world of "jobs for life" with the courage to elevate this event into a turning point. Many of them came in wearing blue suits and stickpins with the bank's logo. In 1996, the bank merged with another financial institution and disappeared. Our graduates moved forward with unexpectedly diverse choices from art leadership, farm ownership, education, and new jobs in emerging industries, and yes, some returned to banking.

One of them was a young man who had become a senior finance executive. He was the first member of his family to go to college. In fact, he had earned an MBA from an Ivy League school. He told us of growing up in a family of migrant workers, doing well in school, and getting a scholarship. But his passion had never been to climb a corporate ladder and make a great deal of money. At one point he whispered to me, "All I ever wanted to do was to grow things." That weekend he designed a whole new life. Today, he is a wealthy farmer growing premium lettuce for gourmet restaurants across the western seaboard.

Another gentleman had come into the program with his wife. He had been with the bank for almost 30 years. Now in his 50s, he panicked about finding another job as a middle-aged man. However, on the second day of the program, his demeanor had changed so completely that I asked what was going on with him. He responded, "I would like to make an announcement to the room." He continued by telling everyone he had always been in love with the world of art and that now he had decided he would "devote the rest of his life to the art community." Years later, I would open up a copy of the *Los Angeles Times* and find his obituary. It read, *"John Morgan, Leader in the Los Angeles Art Community."* He had gone on to open a charity, bringing art education to inner city schools. He raised millions for art museums and he opened up a successful gallery. Later, his wife would share that, for 18 years, "he always left for work with a smile on his face."

I have always been passionate about helping people find new lives and renewed purpose. Some readers might assume that my agenda is to get people to leave their jobs, but that is not the case at all. The vast majority of people want to be inspired and happy in their work. The majority of them find what they are looking for right where they are by simply relating to their circumstances differently. They develop a profound sense of internal drive. It is those who cannot find pleasure and passion in their work who need to leave. Our employers almost always find that those who are most unhappy and disruptive are often those who will never be satisfied. They are in the wrong environment or the wrong role, or both, and they need to go!

In 1990, we were also witnessing a landmark change in the attitudes of America's workers. With the promise of stability shattered, disloyalty was rampant and the press railed on about the inequity of millions of workers being displaced as the coffers of the investment bankers grew exponentially. Human resources professionals complained about the "broken employment contract" and many of us continued to fixate on the losses while a larger wave grew on the horizon. The technology wave would hit our shores and advance so quickly that it would wipe out work as we knew it, and our culture wasn't to blame this time. Still, after almost 300 years, a grieving period seemed in order.

As our early program participants defined and pursued new lives, many of them made a disquieting remark about the great and convulsive change they had just weathered. "I'm glad that's over," they would say. But little did we know that the wave of technology coming towards had only just begun. A few examples:

- Today, a smart phone can monitor a patient's health, predict heart attacks, and directly notify her physician. This technology alone blasts thousands of jobs into the past.

- iPhone cameras are now so sophisticated and produce such superior photographs that an entire class of professional photographers have become obsolete.

- Five years of technological advancement have ended virtually every cashier working on toll roads.

- The last time I used a travel agent was 1998.

- The rate-of-change produced such a need for mentors that an entire coaching industry sprung up overnight. These coaches tell potential clients something like, "If you're nuts, see a therapist. But, if you're healthy, I will help you become more successful without the stigma of working with a psychologist." Many psychologists are only now realizing what these upstarts did to their profession.

As a consumer, picture this: You've wanted that new BMW convertible for quite some time. You get a promotion and a bonus. Your first thought is to order your brand new car. You visit BMW's website and key in all of the options, the color, and the interior; you get to customize this car to fit all your unique design preferences. You click send and the dealership down the block prints out your beautiful new convertible. There is no big factory. There is no shipping. The dealership has no inventory. Does this sound like a pipe dream? In fact, 3D printing has reached such an advanced degree of sophistication that defense contractors are now tooling up to build entire fighter jets without assembly lines.

How will change like this impact our world?

If you are working in a traditional manufacturing setting, it is time to reeducate and reinvent—right now. In the next decade, China will lose the factors that have made it the world's chief manufacturing center and 3D printing is at a tipping point. Most of our leaders don't know it, but the technology has moved well beyond a novelty phase and it is about to go mainstream. GE is ramping up its production of jet engines, medical devices, and home appliance parts using 3D printing, and thousands of other organizations are following suit. Though the direct costs of using 3D technology are often higher, when we add flexibility and remove the need for inventory storage, shipping, and labor, the costs are substantially lower.

I offer up this scenario to portray how much all of us need to learn how to change ourselves. For years, our programs at Inspired Work have given people an active opportunity to change their lives with the endgame being a fulfilled and remarkably effective relationship with their work. So many walk into our programs and tell us, "I can't change. I will be the one person that won't get it." And yet, they walk out the door with new lives. Many of them walk away from crumbling and obsolete platforms.

It's time for us to retire our fixation on what we have lost and instead replace our fear of change with an *enthusiasm for growth*. The new engagement is about learning how to change our focus and behavior rapidly, to let go more quickly, and to anticipate the many roles coming from our future. So when we ask "How the bleep did we get here?" that's how the bleep we got here.

Sadly, huge swaths of the current workforce continue to pine for a return to the past, and this fixation distracts them from the frightening truth that they need to reinvent and transform themselves. But, what if they don't know how? As greater portions of the old workplace disappear, much of America's workforce is standing like frightened deer in the glow of their smartphones. Without meaningful solutions, their pursuit of distraction and numbness only grows. This cultural craving to pursue the safe route, to find predictability somewhere, to get through life with a secure paycheck is obscuring the greatest opportunities for all that we have ever seen before—opportunities to grow with enthusiasm, to celebrate the remarkable change and advancement we are witnessing. We now have the opportunity to jump in and see where the next wave takes us.

This pursuit, my friends, leads to all of us becoming greater, more multi-dimensional human beings. We must stop reacting to the bigger waves by swimming faster, and instead learn how to ride them skillfully. Of course we will continue to experience a sense of awkwardness and some fumbling. That's okay. But as we become skilled in riding the waves, we will find ourselves looking directly into a transformed world. In this new paradigm, mediocre employers will lose their footing. The wise will harness the energy of their brightest workers. The most visionary employers will not only recognize the profit benefits from teaching people how to change, they will help the world make a critical detour from having workers cast to the sidelines as we go. The mentors we develop will not only help our organizations become category leaders, they will become beacons to our community.

For those who learn how to use change as an asset and a resource, the years ahead will be an era where we get to live not just one work life, but rather a variety of lives. We will grow in such unexpected ways that we will become far more interested—and interesting. We will find ourselves creating solutions to all the challenges of this new world around us.

How do I know this is true? Simple. This is how my tribe lives.

So how about we snap out of this trance?

2

A Change of Heart

The global workforce would do well to adopt a new outlook on how we view and respond to change. Given that we are barely keeping up today, consider that emerging technologies in artificial intelligence, life extension, virtual reality, and robotics will continue to redefine how we live, work, and interact with each other. Near-term innovations alone will pave the way for entirely new realities that determine what it means to be productive. And this is just the next wave in an endless sea of future change.

In the face of shorter change cycles, we need organizations that not only help talent embrace new perspectives and life skills, but *require* them to learn and embrace these new essentials. We will need organizations to walk the talk in fostering empathy, collective support, and unification in savvy and strategic ways. The question is, how will we do that in the midst of what appears to so many to be unnerving and tumultuous chaos?

We begin by adopting new mindsets. We need mindsets that can deal with sudden changes and the shoot-from-the-hip responses that too often have kept many workers and organizations stuck in time as the world transforms around them. The old norms are no longer enough. The typical decision-making protocols and reactions must be examined and replaced with actions that are designed to make the best use of each moment. When we expand this challenge to an organizational level, we find out why many of the more progressive organizations do a better job of fostering strong talent in the new environment while the others reach to the past for answers that never satisfy.

Change engenders discomfort always and intense fear frequently. If we are to become artful and skillful in staying ahead of change, it is time to end our resistance to developing what has often been dismissively called "soft skills." In static or stagnant environments, these skills were not viewed as critical. But now, they represent the vitally important skills that enable us to connect with others. This is something we desperately need now. We need these skills to move forward, to get the right information, to find the right help, to build effective support systems, to access high-quality learning and mentorship. Let us explore further what we mean by this.

The Filters of Disengagement

All of us have been trained since birth to wipe out change by using several different filters. We find these filters used often in the workplace to resist change, but they also undermine morale and greater transparency. Effective change requires that we recognize these filters exist in all of us and learn to become aware of them when they are in play. The reactions are often so commonplace and routine that many people assume no one notices the mechanisms involved. Let us start by recognizing and understanding what actually happens when we manage to stop the process of personal change in its tracks.

My core program on work engagement routinely provokes personal change in the compressed period of just two days or 48 hours. This is actually quite remarkable in comparison to other common approaches. In the early days of delivering the programs, a minority of participants would predictably attack our philosophies, which contributed to stress for the facilitators and other participants. But once I defined the filters behind these reactions, we began pointing them out at the beginning of the program, to present them and, thus, get them largely out of our way. For the most part, the outbursts stopped entirely. In our leadership and engagement programs, we also teach people to recognize and manage these "killer filters" so that they are better able to deal with personal and organizational change. So what are these filters? Let's review them here.

Cynicism

Cynicism, most often associated with distrust and pessimism, causes us to question our motivations, undermines our best intentions, and talks us out of taking any action. Cynicism is similar to contrarianism, which is where we always argue the opposite position, even to the most positive mission, vision, and purpose. In the workplace, cynicism shows up in messages like the following:

"We shouldn't be doing this."

"We don't have the time or money to change."

"I don't have the time to learn something new; I'm barely keeping ahead of the work as it is."

In the career development space, it can show up similarly: "I could never make a living doing that."

Contempt

We call this one the "assassination filter." When someone is particularly frightened by change or transparency, they often use a distilled version of cynicism to in order to kill progress and change on-the-spot. It is more intense and drastic.

The Oxford Living Dictionaries' definition of contempt makes the point: "The feeling that a person or a thing is beneath consideration, worthless, or deserving scorn: *he showed his contempt for his job by doing it very badly.*" I often tell leaders that if someone comes after you with contempt, they are more than just fearful; they are terrified.

A few years ago, poet and performance artist Gary Turk created a video called "Look Up,"[1] which quickly went viral. It shows two alternate scenarios. In one version, a young man who is fixated on his cell phone misses the life he was meant to have. In the other version, he "looks up" and meets the love of his life. They marry and raise a family, and he holds her hand in old age as she passes away. Turk's performance piece is a rather eloquent message about what we lose when we "check out" with our technology. To be clear, I don't interpret his video as an attack on technology. Indeed, many are also using it to connect in meaningful ways with others. It is directed towards those of us who become so consumed by technology that we lose out on meaningful human interaction.

Clearly, Mr. Turk's message sparked much contempt when you see some of the reactions:

> "I don't know who I find more galling—Gary Turk, who wrote this one-dimensional preachy fluff, or the millions of sheep sharing it on social media."

> "Thanks Helen! Every time I read it, I just want to rip it apart line by line—I'm glad someone else has the energy to do so."

When an entire team falls into cynicism about a change process, often the most domineering member of that team steps forward with a contemptuous point of view. This is the very indication that we need to educate, comfort, and establish clear messages about our commitment to the change initiative. This also represents a time to point out what people stand to benefit if they get past the filter. People are not motivated much by demands and orders. People tend to get angry when they see their potential but can't find the means to fulfill it. When we give them the insights in how to fulfill their expectations, they do move forward.

Aimlessness

More than 80 percent of America's workers don't like what they do for a living, which means the majority of our workforce is in a state of aimlessness or just going through the motions. They respond to performance commands with contempt. They avoid change because they haven't even defined what they need in their current state, nor are their companies inclined currently to help them define what they really want to do. I have encountered many organizations in which the subtext in the culture is, "If we help them to define what they want to do with their lives, they will leave." How can we possibly produce engagement with this dreadful outlook? Socrates once said, "An unexamined life is not worth living." As we take a closer look at skilled self-inquiry, we begin to realize that becoming aware of these filters also helps us understand the negative impact they have on our individual lives and organizations.

The widespread state of aimlessness is an extension of the malaise that comes from the crash of the Industrial Revolution, as discussed in Chapter 1, but it is also an example of the recruitment pitch we established during that era. We promised people predictability and survival, and many settled for that pursuit. Often, the practice of self-inquiry can be painful because if we "sold out" for predictability and survival, we must face the impact of that decision on our lives and overall well-being. It is no longer enough to simply demand that people "wake up" and show enthusiasm for pushing the organizational vision. We need to get them to define their own highly personalized vision, their own sense of meaning and purpose, and their own compelling definition of what it means to be happy with their work. Until we do this, to varying degrees, we will have drones that drudge along, day after day and year after year.

Resignation

> "I'm too young, too old, too fat, too thin, too stuck, too angry...."

> "I can't take care of my own desires and needs; I have three kids to get through college."

> "We don't have the resources to change, so why should we bother?"

Resignation is the file cabinet that stores all of the "evidence" we have compiled to prove we cannot and will not change.

Some of us would characterize resignation as a lack of hope, but it is actually a lack of optimism, an unwillingness to believe in ourselves or that positive action will make things better. Many times, the experience of failure blossoms into a belief that we simply don't have what it takes to pursue vision or success. Often, we present our problem as a form of bias: "These companies are only hiring young people. You know how it is when you turn 60." That form of resignation overlooks the fact there are scores of people in their 60s, 70s, and even 80s who are making a big difference in the workplace. Resignation is the filter of giving up.

Frenzy

For 20 years, Inspired Work discussed these previous four filters. Societal change, however, has introduced a fifth filter and we call it "frenzy."

According to Dean Schabner of ABC Television, today's full-time employees work an average of 49 hours per week, about six days out of seven days.[2] Since 1993, the average full-time American worker has given up over a month of leisure activity because they are now investing part of the weekend to work. We work harder than any other industrialized nation, including Japan, where workers who used to die from stress received a hero's funeral. About 3.6 million workers in the United States spend more than three hours per day commuting. According to Christopher Ingraham of the *Washington Post*, our annual commute time for just one year, if added up nationally, could have built the Great Pyramid of Giza 26 times over.[3]

Smartphones have opened the door for employers to reach employees at all hours of the day and night. In many cases and with increasing frequency, we are not allowing employees to renew themselves and replenish their energy. France has recognized the problem and even passed a law making it illegal for employers to email employees during off hours.

Many employers mindlessly push people to the edge of crashing and burning. Between commute times, taking care of children, making the mortgage payment, getting groceries, and trying to get enough sleep, frenzy has become a state of mind that shields us from change because we simply don't have the time to reflect on it, let alone pursue it.

• • • • •

How do we deal with these destructive filters?

In our program, we point them out and discuss them; in most cases, that will get them out of the way. Recognize that they reside in all of us and in every organization to some degree. Ask stakeholders to recognize them and help you work through them. Be vigilant. Humans have a particularly creative way of running the filters and biases at a completely unconscious level. Dig into these filters. You then can better anticipate and understand pushback when an announcement of change is made, except you'll be ready for it this time. Understand that identifying, managing, and overcoming these filters are an incredibly valuable skills for your managers and mentors, but also for everyone in the work culture.

Mission, Vision, and Purpose

As we have established, survival and predictability were the primary career standards in the industrial-based past. In that setting, it wasn't necessary to adopt a vision beyond getting a job that provided these basic requirements. This mindset continues to haunt today's workforce to a significant degree and serves to undermine the potential for greater engagement. Additionally, because we now live in a world of constant and accelerating change, we especially need a personal and compelling vision to snap out of the trance, rise above aimlessness, and motivate through the uncertainty and chaos we are now so often finding ourselves in.

During the disruptions of the past few years, most workers didn't see the point of defining personalized vision. However, vision is often the most effective thing to fuel our willingness to change. Without it, we just keep on doing the same things that have thrown people under the bus as the world moves on. It is no longer enough to rely on organizational missions or statements of "what we do here." We are getting lost and we must inspire our people to reconnect with their desires, their will, and their unique voice. We need a way out of the woods.

Many of us laud the extraordinary talent that has driven Apple to become the world's most powerful and masterful consumer products company. Like many other category leaders, it isn't a company that emerged from disengagement. Lore has it that one of the worst or best events that could happen to you as an Apple employee would be to find yourself unexpectedly in an elevator with Steve Jobs. He would ask employees what they were working on and what they were doing. If your response was clear and compelling, your initiative could be immediately funded. If you didn't have much to say, you could be fired by the time the door opened.

Without a clear sense of why we are here personally, relying only on corporate vision to guide our actions results in a high probability that we are not fully present, awake, or deeply involved in our work. We may only get our meaning from somewhere outside our work lives. This is no longer enough to stay in the game successfully. Simply creating shareholder value was never enough. More on this subject shortly.

Transparency = Accountability

Whether we believe it or not, extreme transparency has already been thrust upon us. No one can hide their emails, hide corruption, or hide unhealthy behavior. Transparency has expanded tremendously in the age of sophisticated technologies, and it is delusional for any individual or organization to believe that covertness can be maintained. The most egregious examples of mistreating employees and customers often stem from the belief that no one is watching. Think of all the business and political leaders who have been brought down because they believed no one would find out what they were actually up to. In short, the jig is up.

As the information age advances, many of us have complained about the loss of privacy, but the overall story is actually much bigger and filled with many positive outcomes. We have entered the era of almost total transparency. This reality, by itself, will force our hand and result in vast behavioral changes in how employers are behaving and operating. Clairvoyant CEOs who understand and adapt to this new landscape will reap great rewards. Here is just one example of the new transparency.

Today's savvy employment candidates now often know a great deal about the hiring manager before the first interview—and vice versa. They know his or her reputation, values, and ethics. They know why the last person left the job. They know if the community service initiative is for real or just a stunt designed to check a box. If outsiders have this degree of awareness, consider how quickly actual employees know if a proposed change in the organization is real or just another round of manipulating communications toward phony results. All is revealed through a little electronic sleuthing or advanced social networking, whether it's out by the juice truck or rapid exchanges via text message.

The good news is that this new level of transparency also represents a cornerstone resource for engaging people. Developing full transparency shines a spotlight on all of us. Of course, there may be waves of initial discomfort. It is a bit like pulling everyone out of the closet with all of the attendant awkwardness, fears, and ultimate rewards. I say, bring everyone into the light and stand *with* them. In this new landscape, we no longer ask workers to take on more responsibility without demonstrating the same in ourselves. We should stop demanding that people simply "get used to it." In truth, disengagement has nothing to do with role, rank, or economic power. If CEOs are in fact just as disengaged as the rest of us, what we need is a new model that creates a surging wave of engagement throughout all of us. Trying to hide the truth will only become more difficult with time. Wouldn't it be healthier to build organizations that have nothing to hide, where progress is best achieved when led with stronger ethics and with heart?

Decision Toolbox is one of the world's most innovative recruitment firms. It has more than 100 recruitment professionals tied to state-of-art technology. There are no offices and everyone works from their home. The employees tell the company when they are going to work. The firm has less than 5-percent turnover and has twice received the Alfred P. Sloan Award for Workplace Excellence. One of the fundamental reasons this virtual company is so effective is its complete transparency. Any employee can go online and see the performance metrics for every other employee in the company. These metrics include profitability, accuracy, customer satisfaction, customer loyalty, and speed. This tribal candor leads to collective pride and high quality work. Rather than inspiring fierce competition, the transparency inspires employees to measure up to a team that is one of the best in their industry.

Transparency has also grown in how our leaders communicate. Not long after 9/11, I was asked to design a new leadership program for Disney Consumer Products. At the time, most leadership programs involved sending expensive consultants out to stakeholders to conduct 360 interviews. I felt this rather mindless pattern represented a lost learning opportunity and proposed that we design highly customized 360 assessments by asking the leaders to go out and conduct the interviews themselves. Through the years, organizations often reacted to this idea with shock and the fear that managers would retaliate if given unpleasant feedback or, more likely, that employees would just not be candid. However, we provided a protocol that avoided such outcomes.

Graduates of these very different 360 processes typically told us that it was one of the most life-changing experiences they have had and it occurred from the direct asking and hearing of people's truth. Great leaders also ask great questions and they really listen to the answers. They make it safe to tell the truth. By immersing leaders in this experience and having them directly experience the benefits of candid communication, they can become the kind of modern leaders that effectively deal with change and skillfully connect others to a more collective vision.

Accountability, like transparency, has been a selective force in corporate culture over the years. Without across-the-board accountability, the organization's execution, productivity, and culture always suffer. For example, mid-level managers often continue to pull their own workload while also being responsible for large numbers of workers. The problem is that many are unable to effectively hold their people accountable.

Accountability and transparency are directly linked. We cannot have one without the other. And the lack of them predictably leads to shocking examples of poor quality, low productivity, and bad customer service. Without them, we act like no one will discover the truth and we can get away with all sorts of things. I cannot emphasize enough: it is now totally delusional to believe you can exist without radical transparency moving forward. That is why it is wise to go consider going "all in."

In our programs, the single most common need is for developing managers who live up to new expectations. In the mid-management arena, deepening the breakthroughs in engagement requires significant behavioral change, and it begins with recognizing how frenzy has distracted them from being connected to their workers. In the end, if we want a fully awakened culture, nobody is "off the hook." The bright light must shine on everyone. Living in that light with the kind of integrity that shows we have nothing to hide can bring forth immense power that can fuel new levels of success.

Today's technology offers organizations unprecedented access to employee performance and behavior. If we use it within a truly democratic approach, visibility and transparency become a vital platform for employee engagement.

Value-Driven Cultures

The United States Marine Corps has a leadership development process that isn't just reserved for the high potentials. It is given to everyone. The Executive Council, *Forbes*, and McKinsey have all named the Marine Corps as the number-one leadership organization on the face of the earth. This is because everyone lives by the values of the organization. One of my clients is Mel Spiese, the Major General who led training and development for the U.S. Marines. He prepared more than 300,000 soldiers for combat. When I asked Mel about employee engagement in the Marine Corps, he chuckled and simply said, "Employee engagement has never been a problem for us." I asked Mel if that was because their lives depended on being engaged. He responded, "Sure. But we give everyone the same training, everyone embraces the same values, and because everyone is on the same page, we can trust our lives with the individuals standing next to us."

Everyone is accountable. Everyone "gets it" and everyone buys in. Perhaps most importantly, the Marines teach a series of values that transform anyone, at any level, into a true leader. A values-based culture does not rely on reading a mission statement once or twice per year. Everyone participates in a daily practice of the values and a code of conduct that has essentially developed the Marines into perhaps the most integrity-driven organization anywhere.

Mel says:

> Marines are not born; they are made. They earn the role through practicing our values. The values are identified, codified, taught, and *lived*, in the form of articulated dynamic traits and principles. They become the identity of the individual, and the collective of the individuals, in their practice, becomes the culture of the organization. The identity of the individual and culture of organization are at once synonymous and inseparable. Those values

are ubiquitous throughout—the basis of counsel, development, evaluation, and advancement. They are the unspoken, but clearly understood, expectation of behavior and performance, with the individual and team/unit. More than anything, they link the individual to the institution over time, frankly over the centuries, and are the foundation for individual and organization success under the most demanding of circumstances.

A democracy-based culture implies that everyone is equally responsible. The U.S. Marines is a particularly compelling example because the organization has developed an enduring legacy of building leaders out of individuals many employers would dismiss because they have none of the characteristics of a "high potential." If living by a code can turn someone without a good education and with limited standards into a exemplary leader, why wouldn't any organization run with this relatively simple culture change? Consider how that "non-high-potential" is the same description Mel Spiese uses to describe himself as a young man.

What are the values of an engagement-driven culture? Envision what would happen to your organization if it embraced this code of conduct:

- Routinely engage in self-inquiry to update mission, vision, and purpose.

- Pursue personal change before change impacts you.

- Demonstrate and practice enthusiasm for learning and growth.

- Communicate praise toward colleagues, customers, and direct reports.

- Give high-quality attention to everyone and draw healthy attention to yourself.

- Graciously accept praise from others.

- Tell the truth and seek the truth.

- Support and practice full transparency.

- Foster courage as the correct and healthy response to fear.
- Build effective support systems for success, learning, and feedback.
- When a colleague is frightened, provide comfort and guidance.
- Take nothing personally.
- Help others build the skills for their success.
- Have each other's back.
- Be aware and supportive of your colleague's mission, vision, and purpose.
- No matter what, always be kind.

In essence, values such as these bring about heart in an organization's culture. Heart produces sustainable engagement and has a direct and powerfully positive impact on customers. Heart is our greatest engine. And, it is always already right there, just waiting for the circumstances to come out and flourish.

Our culture is filled with great examples. For years, Southwest Airlines has been recognized for its great customer service and a culture that fosters fun, lightheartedness, and heart. It's even represented in their now-famous logo. In 2013, its CEO, Gary Kelly, realized that it was time to give employees new aspirations, which included the following revisions to their strategic statements: "Our vision is to become the world's most loved, most flown, and most profitable airline.... We exist to connect people to what's important in their lives through friendly, reliable, and low-cost air travel."[4]

Employees of Southwest Airlines are expected to engage in storytelling to reflect how they improve the lives of their passengers by showing interest in their stories and personal lives. In reviewing many of the case studies, I found this letter from a woman named Nancy. She said, "Last night, my husband and I got the tragic news that our three-year-old grandson in Denver had been murdered by our daughter's live-in boyfriend." Her husband had to get to his daughter as quickly as possible. He was on a business trip. In Los Angeles, the crowds were so backed up that he was going to miss the plane. TSA was oblivious, but a flight attendant from the first leg of the journey had already called ahead to the pilot of the last plane. The pilot and ticketing agent were waiting for him. They both said, "Are you Mark? We held the plane for you, and we're so sorry about the loss of your grandson."[5]

This is how it's done.

Mentor-Driven Cultures

With more than two million members, Alcoholics Anonymous, or AA, is the world's largest recovery fellowship. AA has no leaders and little in the form of an organizational structure. And yet, millions of alcoholics and drug addicts have achieved long-term sobriety within its community during the past 80 years. There are two fundamental reasons. First, like the Marines, AA is a values-based program. Everyone that expects to succeed for any length of time is expected to learn and live by the values of recovery. Second, successful program adopters teach the principles and values of the program to the new members. In other words, people who have learned and used "the steps" mentor new people and show them the way. The relationship offers rewards and reinforcement for the mentor and the mentee because it deepens the skills and outlook necessary for long-term success. Employers would do well to pay attention to this example. Why? The model is inexpensive, sustainable, and effective, and it creates a culture of caring.

What can you do right now? Appoint change agents at all levels of the organization. These are individuals not selected for their seniority or functional level. They are selected because they are the successful early adopters of change and engagement. They are naturals. They appreciate the benefits of a new way of working and living. In fact, they are energized by it. Each one can become a valuable coach and mentor to the people around them, perhaps the most valuable.

In smaller organizations, mentors are directly responsible for helping the new people develop, change, and engage with the organization. In larger organizations, we continue to develop mentors but also often provide more formalized learning and change opportunities. Mentors can be particularly powerful in helping colleagues break out of the trance as well as let go of cynicism, contempt, aimlessness, and resignation. They can also identify and help resolve skill deficits. As with a 12-step program, mentors are equally susceptible to falling behind, but with healthy, intact teams mentors will also be supported by their colleagues.

In other words, reverse mentoring is also encouraged. For example, when an intact team participates in one of our Inspired Work programs, most become more compassionate as they hear firsthand about the hopes, dreams, aspirations, and challenges of their colleagues. When we dissolve the silos and separation, we produce stronger relationships and the human heart emerges easily. It shows up when we have each other's backs.

Creating cultures like this require courage, they require everyone's participation and accountability, and they require the kind of heart-driven actions that awaken almost everyone. When we encounter those rare individuals who are beyond reaching, it may be time to set them free. Do not allow them to thwart the positive progress and momentum. Make your environment transparent. Foster skills and behaviors that don't allow any reason to hide. Empower everyone who has already changed to help others catch up. Give them the life-infusing skills and expect the best from them.

3

The Art of Change

Personal change can be one of the most frightening of human experiences. It often requires letting go of old beliefs, behaviors, outlooks, and sometimes even our friends and jobs. At the very least, engagement requires thorough self-examination of obsolete truths. Is it still true? Does this outlook still serve me?

For example, there are quite a few parents who believe their children should set aside their real ambitions by going to college and getting a "real job." Is that belief system still true? Letting go of that belief system introduces some parents' greatest fears about their children's well-being and future. Successful personal change thrives when people help each other. In isolation, most workers cannot even articulate what actually frightens them about change.

Artfully changing our lives and organizations requires that we respond to fear in healthy and positive ways. For many, to fluidly find and listen to the truth, and to skillfully reinvent our lives, requires a reinvention in how we view and respond to fear. In our culture, fear is ridiculed and demonized, yet we still experience it. Self-help gurus promise that if we take their course, we will overcome fear, but it is still there. Behavioral scientists have identified the purpose of fear is to take action, and yet so many of us are conditioned to not take action when we are frightened. The conditioning that has led many Americans to use inaction when frightened has led to large swaths of our culture into creative thinking, which is only the first half of real creativity. Creative thinking isn't creativity until we take action. Unfortunately, those of us who fear the risk action requires end up running from the very actions that will change our lives and our organizations.

In a culture fixated on security, we have reinforced the myth that there is something fundamentally inadequate about us when we feel fear. If that is the case, we construct our lives around avoiding fear, and as a result, the real and best opportunities don't even reach our field of vision. All of this strange ideology disappears as we cross a street and a large truck roars around the corner. As it heads directly towards us, our biology takes over. An alarm goes off that pours powerful hormones and chemicals into our body. This system is perfectly designed for pushing us into action. Why does our culture need to make up so many strange stories and myths that contradict basic biology?

One of the most famous quotes of all time is Franklin D. Roosevelt's "The only thing we have to fear is fear itself." We sent more than 17 million Americans into World War II. I have yet to find any of those soldiers' stories repeating the president's missive. On the other hand, we find countless narratives in which those in the frontlines characterized the experience as the single most terrifying event in their lives. In some cases they did hide. In others they shot first. In all cases, they took action.

Perhaps a healthier alternative statement would be, "The only thing have we to fear is to forget courage." True courage isn't about walking into difficult situations as a robot devoid of feelings. As a famous male icon of that era, the brutish John Wayne, once said, "Courage is being scared to death, but saddling up anyway."[1]

Cher has experienced lifelong crippling bouts of stage fright. She tells journalists that it is as bad today as it was in her 20s. Early on, she depended on Sonny Bono to get her on stage and keep her grounded. Today, she deals with it by hiring stage managers who, if needed, drag her to the stage door. Once on stage, that previously terrified woman, in an instant, becomes Cher.[2]

I mentioned previously how some groups that I worked with in the early days would get into debates about whether our discussion concerned a vision, a mission, or a purpose. This discourse would detour us from defining a new game that would put everyone into action and hence risk. So, I told them to use all three. Similarly, rather than debating whether we should overcome fear, include fear, or avoid fear, let's move the organizational culture forward by making it okay to be frightened (or not), but always rewarding others for courage. Promote courage. Make courage a vital part of the organizational ethos.

Our dysfunctional responses to fear erode change and engagement. If someone is afraid to look customers in the eye, how can they connect? If a leader is afraid to look at the truth, how will employees trust they can live out their personal ambitions? If a CEO is afraid to stand for value, how can the company foster it? If we continually pine for a simpler past, how can we possibly learn how to build our future? What is it that frightens us about change?

This is what I have learned.

A few years after we began Inspired Work, a series of insights emerged from observing our participants. As they designed compelling change within their lives, our participants had to consistently work through a series of obstacles. Our participants come from every walk of life, but this quest to change brought up fear and discomfort in literally every participant. These challenges can impact many if not all of us.

From the time that we commit to change, we begin a journey that includes four distinct events. Each event has a tendency to be more frightening than the previous step. Embedded in a successful journey through each event is a series of life skills that are learnable. Consequently, many of our participants realize their ambitions by developing the skills. Building these skills within any workforce represents a relatively straightforward and simple exercise. The skills elevate our individual and organizational capacity to change to one of finesse and perhaps even artfulness.

Some of the skills we will examine have been dismissively called "soft skills." Why? These are often the very skills that require a degree of courage to use and to learn. As we proceed, I propose we aptly name them "courage skills." When we examine these skills carefully, we find the very tools that help us to connect with the world around us.

As addressed previously, meaningful change begins with a compelling and personalized vision. This is the fuel that drives people to move forward. One of the primary reasons surveys are greeted by the employees with cynicism is that questions are often skewed towards supporting the corporate vision without any interest in hearing what employees want to accomplish.

One of the breakthroughs in this solution will be found in insisting on both strong organizational and individual visions. As robots become part of every workplace, we will not be looking for humans to continue exhibiting the robotic behavior we created during the Industrial Revolution. Getting there requires that we understand the mechanisms in which we commonly trip up and the skills that will help us sail through change. Once activated, the overall process of self-change is learnable and can be sold to all workers. But first, test the processes yourself. I don't want you to sell something you haven't embraced. Like learning to play the piano, it can begin with the awkward attempts to play scales and simple pieces of music. Stick with it, work with it, and become artful in changing life for the better.

Without the fuel of vision, there is no reason to go through the discomfort and work associated with personal change. In this chapter, we are going to examine the real reasons we are afraid of change and how to get through the events that cause those fears. To succeed with change, all that it takes is an open heart, a dose of courage, and the willingness to learn new skills.

Successful change is based on a journey that includes four events. Each event has a tendency to be more frightening than the previous step. We master each step through understanding, motivation, and skill building.

Let's begin with the first step. Consider the possibility that all of us know, on some fundamental level, that when we commit to personal change, we step onto a road that will include a series of progressive challenges. We can easily keep off this road by using three magic words. For example, ask someone the question, "What do you want to do with your life?" Bets are pretty high someone will respond, "I don't know." These three words represent the end of the conversation, and unless we persist in answering the question, they are off the hook. In our culture, we seem to have a collective interest in protecting this "out." When we use the words, people rarely, if ever, challenge the statement.

Step 1: Commit

"I don't know."

How do we get past this obstacle? Retire the words. "I don't know" is no longer a good enough answer. Ask everyone to dig and never settle. Your organizational mentors will be asked to send an employee that offers this out to go back and answer the question. It is a fact that all of us have our own truth. Establish cultures where everyone's truth is defined and told. Without this one transaction, you have an organization filled with "I don't know" and this is one of the first seeds of disengagement.

We don't need to build cultures that scare people into engagement. However, leadership needs to make it clear that we will not accept "I don't know" as an answer about one's mission, vision, and purpose. These three words protect "the trance." Let's build cultures where everyone is connected to the answer. If it is out of sync with the organization's mission, vision, and purpose, take the initiative to connect them. Today's leaders need to skillfully knit the two together.

Step 2: Declare Our Vision

"You're crazy."

Everything of value in our culture is a collaborative experience. If that is difficult to ponder, consider that all of us are here because two people collaborated. Let's agree that our next step is to declare our vision. Who do we tell first? Usually, we begin by telling members of our tribe. The problem is, tribes have rigid rituals and expectations, and when we break those rituals, they generally respond with some form of "You're crazy." For example, let's say that we go home to the spouse and declare, "I'm going to leave the six-figure job that I can do in a coma. In fact, I'm going to start a business that is altruistic in nature." What will the spouse say? In an alternate scenario we call a meeting with our coworkers and tell everyone, "I know the budget has been slashed by 40% but you know what? Today, we are committing to a business revolution." You guessed it, they are going to think and say, "You're crazy."

In the natural progression of articulating a vision and bringing it to life, we begin by telling someone, and usually that someone is a member of our tribe.

Welcome to the second step.

Many of us don't really think about the power that tribes have on our lives. Whenever we belong to a tribe, we are making an agreement to play by the rules of that tribe. This is the essence of belonging. Tribes include families, employers, religions, political parties, social groups, and community groups. The power of belonging to a tribe cannot be underestimated. Author Seth Godin said, "It turns out that tribes, not money, not factories, that can change our world, that can change politics, that can align large numbers of people. Not because you force them to do something against their will. But because they wanted to connect."[3] Of course we want to connect! This dynamic also implies how important it is for employers to become the tribe of choice. The dark side of the goodness of tribes is they do have rigid rituals, expectations, and influence that can keep many of us fully stuck.

Los Angeles is a city of tribes with thousands of groups adopting distinct rituals, values, and expectations. I have three styles of suits, two types of sport coats, and two forms of casual wear, all so I can be respectful when I visit client sites. None of them appreciate my showing up in the wrong costume. I've been told, "Leave the tie in the car," "Wear a jacket," and "You look like one of us."

The pressures of tribes on career choices are legendary. During a particularly large public program, we had about a dozen men come back from lunch laughing. They had defined the Jewish mother's hierarchy of acceptable career choices. It was all based on how one mother reacted when the other shared what her son did for a living. There were three acceptable choices and each one provoked varying levels of enthusiasm. A minor rise of the eyebrows was CPA. Halfway up the forehead was attorney. To the hairline? Of course, it was doctor. A specialist provoked a natural facelift.

One of those sons went home and announced he was leaving his legal practice to become a florist. How do you think they responded? I am just kidding when I share that one aunt cracked an egg over her head.

Sadly, our tribe often reacts to a new mission, vision, and purpose with the default reactions of pushback. It isn't a particularly conscious way to react as it is usually driven by fear. Of course, it is easy for us to react with righteousness and anger. Our loved ones are supposed to support us. Our colleagues are the ones who ought to understand. Our spouses should be happy and back our new ideas. But this is not how human beings process change. Human beings are hard-wired to think of something other than themselves for a maximum of *15 seconds*. This means that when we make a declaration of change, the tribe wonders how it is going to impact them or their fears about us. My good friend Tom Drucker launched the Xerox Sales Institute in the early 1980s. Faced with global competition for the first time, Xerox hired a cadre of behavioral scientists to study the psychology of selling. This is where they identified the 15-second process, which turned pitch-selling on its head. People are not interested in our resumes. They are not interested in our declarations. People are focused on one thing and that is fulfilled expectations. Today's better sales professionals don't make pitches; they ask great questions. The best of our modern leaders are inquisitive and constantly finding the needs and expectations of their stakeholders. Tribes have a tendency to be more receptive when we make the declaration in ways that fit the tribe's needs and expectations. We increase our probability of success by managing these tribal responses. Also, a new mission can often require the needs of an additional tribe or moving altogether.

Here are a few examples of speaking or not speaking to expectations:

(Self-Indulgent Version)

"You know what? I'm quitting the law firm on Monday and going to cash in my stock to start a business of my own. I'm buying that florist shop on the corner. You're upset? Why can't you be happy for me?"

(Tribe-Friendly Version)

"I have an announcement to make. For the last ten years, I've been bringing all of this negative energy to our gatherings. You have become used to my unhappiness with practicing law. So, I'm pursuing work where I can have more freedom and get out of endless, mentally strenuous days. I'm buying that florist shop on the corner and my commitment is to show up to the family with a smile on my face and flowers in my hands."

(Self-Indulgent Version)

"Profits have been sinking for a long time. So today, we launch a business revolution. All of you are going to bring one actionable innovation to me by the end of the month and we are going to pull out of our nosedive. Now, get back to work."

(Tribe-Friendly Version)

"Many of you are uncomfortable with the cutbacks and the downturn in the market. I was sad to see so many people leave. But, you are here and you are here for a reason. I am asking that everyone works on one actionable innovation and have it ready by the end of the month. If we create a business revolution, all of us are going to have more to work with, we will have more security, and we will look back on this period as a turning point, one that we remember with pride. My commitment to you is this experience will help all of us grow."

The problem that many of us have with change is that we don't really think about the impact and the influence of tribes on our decisions and commitments, especially when it involves a change in the tribe's beliefs. Sometimes, we hide the commitment so we don't have to deal with the pushback. Often, a colleague is sitting right next to coworkers, withholding a breakthrough because he is concerned with the cynicism and contempt that would get showered on him for speaking up.

How do we treat the problem?

Giving consultative sales training to every member of our team is a beginning. This is the sales process in which we don't make a pitch but ask the questions that help us define the needs and expectations of the other people. When all of us learn how to find the needs and expectations of others, every aspect of organizational performance improves. Encourage people to speak up, to declare, to share vision and innovation.

As a leader, there is also great value in defining the tribe. For example, employer brands are just as important as consumer brands. When top-tier students graduate from Stanford, the holy grail of tech education, they will consider Apple, Google, and entrepreneurship. How many will think of Yahoo as an employer of choice? A tech organization's success begins with the quality of talent it attracts, develops, and retains. The best have clearly defined employer brands, one that has become embedded in their heads. That requires consistency in the message and full truth in the definition. Years ago, I was in the midst of a leadership program at Disney. One of the executives asked me what I thought Disney's employer brand could be. I responded, "To create magic at great profit in the midst of chaos." Gasps and laughter ensued. I don't know where it came from but I still believe this is the culture of Disney. Here is a company that has become an indelible consumer brand throughout the world. There have also been mixed messages about Disney as an employer with some ex-workers referring to the organization as "Mousewitz." Here's why: For someone who loves creating magic at great profit in the midst of chaos, Disney is a dream employer. People who love this mission have often worked there for 20 and 30 years. On the other hand, if someone isn't enthused about the brand, it will be an unhappy ride.

The challenges around declaring our mission or our commitment are learnable. The value of thoroughly defining the tribe raises the probability of "right fit" with our employees and also helping others remain accountable to the tribal needs. Becoming skilled in managing tribal reactions is one of the keys to anyone's overall success.

Step 3: Draw Healthy Attention to Ourselves

"They'll hurt me."

Our third step introduces new levels of challenge. In order to grow our vision, we have to draw healthy attention to ourselves. In our culture, this very necessary and ongoing action is often thwarted with the message, "They'll hurt me."

Fear of visibility has been with us for thousands of years. Out in the jungle, being visible could have dire consequences. In the jungle of business, visibility might turn us into a target.

Quite simply, as we increase our visibility, we also increase the risk of getting hurt. But, it is equally true that when we decrease our visibility we also increase our risk of starving. Consequently, many people have developed just enough visibility to get by, but certainly not enough to thrive. In a world where change accelerates every day, the need to draw attention towards us also grows. Because within the world of change, we have to connect with others, we have to be seen, we have to get others to helps us identify the pathway towards the next bridge, and most of us need mentors to shine lights on our blind spots. If we are "flying below the radar" no one will know we are there and change is ruthless to anyone who hides. Returning to the topic at hand, isn't it common sense that someone who is hiding from attention is also disengaged?

During the Industrial Revolution, visibility was reserved for sales professionals. The rest of us did what was expected, which was about completing tasks without getting attention. In the modern world, growing transparency gives us no place to hide. Increasing change means having to remarket ourselves in continual ways. As the world speeds up, learning how to give attention to others also becomes a critical and much-needed life skill. Though this move might seem counterintuitive, the world's greatest futurists and organization development leaders tell us that as software and technology takes over logic-based work, the growth opportunities will go to those of us who are strongly empathetic, communicative, influential, gifted storytellers, and able to sell concepts.

The ability to draw attention to ourselves represents a broad set of skills. It is a bit like comparing someone who can drive a car to an individual who is a very good owner of a car. Driving is but one skill. Learning how to select the right car, get the appropriate insurance, maintain it properly, and make sure all of the passengers are safe represents a series of skills, and this is what most workers need if they are to engage, connect, succeed, reinvent, unlearn, and relearn. Without these varied skills attached to attention, we fail because of isolation. In my work with helping people change their relationship towards work, I find that isolation is central to most everyone's failure.

The challenge of isolation and being starved for attention reaches all the way up to CEOs. In many cases, senior management and owners fail because they cannot establish enough muscle or safety to disclose what they don't know. We hide our inadequacy and create the delusion of adequacy only to find ourselves jailed in an obsolete playbook.

This isolation is a natural extension in how we lived during the last 30 years of the 20th century. In the 1980s, Alice March, the executive director of Focusing Awareness on Children and Television, conducted in-depth studies about the impact of television on American families. She discovered the average family spends seven minutes a day communicating, four of those minutes are simply commands or requests. That same family goes on to watch television for approximately four hours per day. This means the modern family is no longer an effective laboratory for learning how to draw healthy attention to oneself or give it to others.

In 1990, Barry Levinson produced a movie called *Avalon*. In it, an immigrant family comes to America in the early 20th century and builds a small furniture business in Baltimore. Every night, they gather around the table and discuss the day, argue, gossip, and get into each other's business. One day, the patriarch of the family comes home with a wooden box.

He proclaims, "We are going to make a fortune selling this."

"This" is was one of the first television sets. In the next scene, the family has moved from the dining room to the living room and they are staring vacantly at the box. The movie closes one generation later in the mid-1960s. Two of the children are now parents with their kids.

They sit behind individual TV trays looking at a show. They have forgotten each other. They are learning absolutely nothing about the value and need for attention.

Perhaps the baseline in our culture is that most of us have inadequate skills for drawing healthy attention towards ourselves and giving it to others. But when we take individuals who grew up around violent attention, the barrier towards learning the skills is much steeper. Of course, there will be discomfort in learning the skills, but on the other side of the learning experience is a more confident and effective life. We become more visible, we sell our good ideas, we pay better attention to our colleagues, we become more at ease in expressing our needs, and we look our customers and coworkers in the eye. These are the skills that few American families are building within their children. Schools are not performing a much-needed intervention. When we reach the workplace, isn't it ironic that the very skills workers need to be able to change, connect, engage, and reinvent are branded as "soft skills"?

About 500 yards from our home is a grocery store, part of a big national chain. Every time that I go into that store, there are several cashiers and baggers who will not look me in the eye or connect in any meaningful way. The only reason that we go there is because it is next door. Every time that I see them, I wonder what the story is. Who bullied that person? What happened in his family? Why doesn't the manager take her under wing and start an intervention? I can't help but think of our capacity to hurt others so deeply that they have trouble looking a customer in the eye. But these interactions happen every single day and they happen because no one had the heart to intervene and change the legacy. Unfortunately, until these workers are given an intervention, they will also turn off their customers eight hours a day.

Intervening with this deep-seated fear of attention is a matter of business, profits, happy customers, and loyal colleagues. Helping our workers open up and connect is not only life-changing, but when we extend it to all workers, it is game-changing.

In an upcoming chapter, we will outline how to build this skill in everyone.

Step 4: Build Effective Support Systems

"Sounds good. What is it?"

We have arrived at the final step that is the most important ingredient for a healthy workplace, an effective career, and a joyful life. Truly successful people have highly diverse and effective support systems. Many workers don't define what they really want because, at an often unconscious level, they assume they will not find the support needed to bring that vision to life. Make no mistake: the vision is still there. A true and inspired vision or dream never dies. However, when hidden, it festers. When we operate with a submerged vision, we fall into some degree of malaise, and the job becomes more of a drain than a joy. The trance takes over. But, once we do define our vision, our success is based *purely* on the quality of our support systems. Therefore, our ability to build support systems is perhaps the single most important skill in becoming successful.

Year in and year out, *Fortune* magazine publishes its famed 100 Best Places to Work edition. A central theme with organizations that stay on this list for years is a surprise to many. All of them consciously foster strong relationships amongst their employees.[5] When two employees form a strong bond, that relationship becomes a new asset within the organization. These relationships lead to more innovation, increased productivity, and strong morale; when the chips are down, that relationship might be the one asset that motivates them to stay and resolve the problems. It may also occur in the form of someone bonding with an outside entity. This new support system can become yet another asset for the employer by bringing in valuable intelligence, new business, and needed innovation. For example, I find that when we give social networking training to human resources, the team brings the outside world in. They access new talent pipelines, mentors, and business intelligence, and become more effective in building their individual careers.

When we do define a vision, *success is based solely on the quality of our support systems.* For most workers, this is a counterintuitive idea until it finally sinks in. In the old work model, we got punished if we asked for help. It distracted us from plugging bolts in holes and filling quotas. Now, the ability to build effective support systems is the single most important skill in becoming successful with change. The importance of these support systems only grows as the world speeds up. For many, shifting gears in this area will provoke discomfort. In the industrial-based work world, asking for help was viewed as a sign of weakness. Today, it is not only necessary, support systems are the single most important assets that help us change and adapt as the world moves forward. Showing all of your workers how to build support systems and holding them accountable to do that within and outside of the organization will transform your culture.

New support systems can introduce unexpected miracles into the lives of employees. Years ago, I was working with a management team that was facing huge organizational change and daunting competitive challenges. At one point, an executive became emotional and disclosed that she was trying to have a child and that her stress level was so high that her hope of becoming a parent was dissolving. Her colleagues started taking on some of her work to support her. Months later, I was sitting in the lobby of her building. She happened to walk in. We looked at each other and the tears welled up. She was wearing a maternity dress. We hugged. That turning point elevated the lives of her colleagues as well. There are so many myths out there about successful organizations also being ruthless employers; the common belief is that when a woman becomes a mother, the fast track is over. We hear about employers curtailing a person's future because they stop giving up their life for the job. However, I find it is the organizations that allow employees to develop in all areas of life that sustain success and growth.

Helping a colleague develop insights around the need and value for support systems can change their lives. This past year, a young man was sent to me to discuss his difficulties in getting a film deal. He is a devoted father and his family comes first. He was seriously considering dropping out of the film business and going into a more "practical" line of work. But the quality of his film work was world class. Unfortunately, his support system was almost nonexistent. He had a notion that it was unmanly to ask agents, producers, and studio executives for help. We threw all of our energies into developing a personal brand and developing a solid support system. Within three months, the Sundance Film Festival picked up his first film. Today his career is skyrocketing. Instead of being someone's gopher, he has a skilled assistant of his own.

Mentorship is one of the purest forms of building high-quality support throughout an organization, leading to employees become more supportive of the organization. Customers can feel it. We teach our employees to practice courage when we learn how to draw effective attention to ourselves and to give it to others, to look each other in the eye, and to ask someone to help with the problems that matter to us the most. Perhaps, if we work hard, our renewed workplace becomes the home that prepares us for the future of work.

It doesn't get better than that.

• • • • •

Learning how to navigate these steps represents a fundamental beginning towards helping each and every employee to change and engage with the world around us. As they learn, the beginning might feel counterintuitive. Perhaps some will say they don't have the time to work on anything other than their work. But as they do become involved, more will be revealed, the path will become clear, and they will see how important it is to reinvent and stay ahead of the waves. They will help each other and as they do, the culture turns into something new. The culture won't become soft. Transparency will become a positive tool for engagement. But more than anything, results will create a new enthusiasm that builds the mission and provides multiple new dimensions to the culture. All will be sustained because everyone is engaged and everyone is accountable.

4

Mission, Vision, and Purpose: Fuel for Change

"Beware the barrenness of a busy life."

—Socrates

Effective personal change begins with a vision, mission, and purpose that are personal, meaningful, and absolutely real. When these elements are intact, translating vision into reality is one of the most transformative of all human experiences. The journey you must take to get there elevates lives, both your own and those of the people around you, and orchestrates your growth along the way. Without a clearly defined personal mission, vision, and purpose, we operate in a state of relative aimlessness and barrenness. We begin to wither, and the resulting trance perpetuates the notion that a fulfilled vision is simply out of our reach. The added frenzy supports the idea that we don't even have time to look at what we want out of our lives. It's a self-reinforcing trap, and we lose the skills of self-inquiry that can lead to meaningful insights, personal change, and staying competitive.

We must understand that defining and connecting to all that are precious and meaningful to us raises our motivation to an entirely new level. Establishing purpose brings clarity to our day-to-day living. Though the value of developing a strong organizational mission, vision, and purpose is drummed into business leaders throughout their professional lives, far less emphasis is placed on the need for personalized mission, vision, and purpose, if at all. Instead, much lip service is given to the idea of employees needing to get behind the mission, vision, and purpose of our organizations. Yet we are not as conditioned to ask our employees what *they* want out of life, what *they* wish to accomplish, and what is precious and meaningful to *them*. This isn't done maliciously, but mindlessly. Despite the fact that business leaders such as Stephen Covey promoted personal vision, the behavior of most organizations demonstrate that a person's personal vision, mission, and purpose doesn't matter. And this is how we've lived for more than 300 years.

In the game of employee engagement, how far has this pursuit taken us? Nowhere. The minute we ask employees to adopt and support the company vision without even inquiring about their personal vision, we step back into the old miserable paradigm that implies a "do it or else" mandate. With decades of moving employees around like numbers, what kind of cynicism and contempt can you imagine comes up when we ask people to buy into a vision that in many cases is only about raising shareholder value?

Maya Angelou's missive, "I've learned that people will forget what you said, people will forget what you did, but people will never forget how you made them feel,"[1] is relevant in your own organization. When we dismiss someone's vision, they will likely give up on it. George Washington Carver was born into slavery but became our country's most influential botanist and inventor. In 1941, *Time* magazine placed Mr. Carver on the cover and referred to him as "America's Black Leonardo DaVinci."[2] Carver said, "When there is no vision, there is no hope."[3] By ignoring the deepest seeds of meaning and purpose in our employees, we actually contribute to setting the stage for barrenness in their lives.

Great leaders recognize that stakeholders become engaged when we help them access what they most want out of their work, their lives, and their careers. Well, it is the same for our employees. And as we develop the skills of self-inquiry, the process becomes both lighter and enlightening. Time and time again, we find that a large portion—if not the majority—of America's talent at some point settled for what they got over what they wanted. We have become so busy that the purpose that would drive us forward, that would inspire us to be our very best, only sits quietly until the self-inquiry begins.

A fully engaged workforce can only be attained when we nourish dual vision. In a transparent environment, it is perfectly okay for individual vision to be defined, expressed, and fulfilled, even if it ultimately leads to someone's departure. We are then able to support each other in pursuing the lives we want, lives that are as personalized and as clearly defined as a fingerprint. We are also better able to discuss our fears of falling out of step with change. These discussions will lead to solutions. When we develop this kind of clarity in working with one another, we become more willing to experience the discomfort associated with re-invention and change.

Organizational vision, mission, and purpose are critical to building a strong brand. However, strong engagement requires that we take this a step further by giving just as much energy to helping our employees realize their vision and encouraging them to fulfill their dreams. Starbucks has done a better job than most. The company's mission is "[t]o inspire and nurture the human spirit—one person, one cup, and one neighborhood at a time."[4] The company has taken interest in its employees' personal mission, vision, and purpose by offering one of the most comprehensive educational assistance programs in the world. Not surprisingly, Starbucks has also become a home for some of our most engaged and talented workers. People can go there to, in part, fulfill their ambition to be educated. They even go so far as to provide counselors that can give academic guidance.

For most organizations, one of the first steps that can be taken towards building a vital and effective culture is to give equal importance to the mission, vision, and purpose of their employees. They can do this by establishing environments that not only listen but also actively encourage colleagues to clearly articulate what they want to do—for example, "I want to become such a strong graphic artist that I can become a creative director, either here or someplace else." The overall approach can be as simple as shifting from statements like "Get to work" to "What do you want to get out of working here?" The latter actually establishes an inner thought process that leads to good outcomes for both parties and gives the boss information that, when properly managed, can motivate and inspire more from the employee.

I've watched participants in my programs define the lives they want to have and then commit to removing anything that is in their way. I've watched unhappy parents redefine their lives and become role models to their children. I've observed workers who were causing everyone around them to be miserable make amends and finally deal with the wounds of their past. And I've watched narcissistic executives become inclusive leaders. *None of these transformations took place by adopting someone else's vision.* It happened when they looked within themselves and defined who they wanted to be in their relationships with work, life, and the world around them.

Developing work environments that included robust self-inquiry would have been completely out of place in the Industrial Revolution. Many leaders even today will respond with contempt to the idea of developing self-inquiry with all of their workers. They have no frame of reference or context for it. But times and contexts have changed dramatically. How will we motivate workers to change and engage if we are not developing environments with *shared* vision? In order to develop this capability, the more intelligent organizations will be the ones in which its leaders explore three questions with all employees:

1. What is your vision?
2. What is our vision?
3. How can we weave the two together?

Perhaps it would be valuable to tell you where my self-inquiry began. I have sought personal and spiritual growth my entire adult life. Many of the programs and quests that I experienced were exciting and wonderful at the time. But the impact wore off because we were engaged in rituals and experiences that were based on someone else's truth and methodology. For example, if someone's idea of joy and excitement is camping, they may think everyone ought to love camping, right? But bring the topic up to me and I will head for the doors. Many of our most hallowed expectations have been based on someone's idea that a certain philosophy and set of values would improve everyone's life. But when one point of view is pushed on others, there's bound to be contention between its values and that of the individual. Far-reaching and deep-seated questions, however, can lead us to our individual truth and our individual path.

I discovered the Socratic approach through Dr. Cherie Carter-Scott, MCC, the author of *If Life Is a Game, These Are the Rules: 10 Rules for*

Being Human and the founder of MMS Institute, a coach training organization founded in 1974. For more than four decades, Cherie and her sister Lynn have conducted Inner Negotiation Workshops that pose questions to participants. When I experienced their work, I realized that asking people the right questions and encouraging them to answer the questions is perhaps the single most effective way to produce sustainable change. This is because the answers are based on the individual's personal truth. It is also the most respectful approach because it recognizes that *we* are the experts of our own lives. In Socratic work, every outcome is unique because everyone's truth is highly individual.

One of the biggest turning points in my life came not long after experiencing the Socratic process. A well-known producer who was launching a new record label contacted me; he wanted me to become the first artist on his new label. I had worked towards that moment for 12 years. The day that I joined the staffing industry was also the day that I made a commitment to work on my career as a musician. I didn't want to struggle in road bands or play in bars. All that I wanted was a recording deal, session work, and concert tours. I worked towards this goal diligently, playing original music in small clubs and slowly working up to greater venues. With that one phone call, I felt that my ship had come in.

A few weeks after we started the project, however, I received another call. My producer had just dropped dead of a heart attack. In that one moment, given the dramatic example this represented for me, I realized that I had devoted much of my adult life to being happy *sometime in the future*. This opened the door to the sobering reality that I knew little of value about being happy in the moment and in the present. When I began exploring how to redesign my life to experience happiness on a day-to-day basis, it hit me that I would also have to reinvent the way I related to my work life. In fact, it became clear that for most of us, work is the biggest relationship that we have. It is, after all, where we spend most of our waking adult hours, and if we have a mediocre relationship with out work, we probably have a mediocre overall experience of life by default. Not that everything is mediocre, but that this one very important part of life can have an overall and cumulative effect on one's whole life experience.

I had brief indications before of what my ideal life's work could be. A few years prior, I was in a four-day intensive workshop with about 100 other participants. Right in the middle of it, I realized I could design a far more effective program with better results in half the time, but I didn't entertain the thought much. In fact, I took a momentary look at it and put it as far out of my head as humanly possible. Changing other people's lives, after all, was not on my righteous agenda. In fact, I had a spiritual leader approach me and tell me that I ought to be helping other people find the lives they are meant to have. I didn't respond kindly or with any sense of receptivity.

I recount this story because some people will initially run from their true mission, vision, and purpose. I discounted what I was born to do. My insistence on music and what my life was supposed to look like shielded me from my own truth. In the years since then I have witnessed this same process happening in thousands of people who have attended my workshops. What I learned is that we often live in blind spots because we are conditioned to believe in one set of ideals and these ideals are often not our own.

The next turning point for me began one morning when I was sitting on the beach and pondering the unhappiness I was experiencing with my career. I had planned on leaving the staffing industry for a record contract. Because I had spent so much time looking to the future for happiness, I was distracting myself from the fact that I didn't really like my work. I didn't like the aggressive nature of the environment I managed on the owner's behalf. I didn't like moving people from one job to the next without any significant consideration for the impact on their lives outside of making a bit more money and getting a little more praise from my boss. I didn't see the meaning and purpose of it all except for the fact that I made a lot of money. It dawned on me that most of my friends and colleagues were in the same boat. Ironically, many people considered me to be an expert about work!

That morning, I dug my toes into the sand and thought about the legacy of a life's work. It hit me that the Industrial Revolution gave us a series of standards and behaviors that we had used for almost 300 years. That meant that approximately 10 generations had passed those principles down to the present time. Being the good recruiter that I was, I asked myself, "So, what was the promise? What did we offer to people that inspired them to join the cubicles and workstations and to spend hours, days, months, and years there?" It was predictability and survival. It's no wonder that so many of us have a mediocre experience of work. If predictability and survival are what we bought as the purpose of work, what happens to meaning, purpose, joy, contribution, wild success, and making a difference? These characteristics would be irrelevant in that worldview. So I wondered what kind of world existed beyond these two relatively mediocre standards. A two-word phrase came up in my mind: "irrevocable happiness."

Irrevocable means "can't be taken away." What would our lives look like if we were, in essence, sentenced to happiness? We would be living on our own terms with our own standards and our own definition of purpose. Every person's definition would be unique. I asked myself what my own irrevocable happiness was. As I wrote down my answers to this question, I realized that some of my standards had always been there but had never been examined. Some of my words completely surprised me. I wrote, "I would only work with brilliant and loving people." I had absolutely no evidence this was possible, but it was what I wanted. I wanted brilliant. I wanted individuals who would push me to grow in ways I could never anticipate. I wanted people that had such good hearts and souls that I loved them and they would freely love me. This is how I live today. These are the people who work with me and surround me. That one sentence became a standard that changed my life.

I also wrote, "I would change people's lives in lasting and meaningful ways." This was a surprising disclosure. That day on the beach was the point where I realized that I threw away that moment in the seminar because I could actually see how to get people to transform their work, elegantly and eloquently.

I had observed many people stand up and make grandiose announcements because of the standards imposed on them by the curriculum, such as "Make a difference." None of them offered sound principles for how to implement making a difference. It hit me on that day that most of us need far more effective means of insight and support to define work based on our own unique definition of spiritual, emotional, and practical DNA.

In the years since, thousands of our participants have written out their own definition of irrevocable happiness. Every interpretation is different and unique. Consider for a moment that our overreliance on assessments plays to the notion that we don't know who we are. Therefore, many of our employees continue to buy into the idea that self-knowledge is elusive and mysterious. This position weakens us and diminishes our personal power. A solid Socratic process dispels this because we are helping people—some for the first time ever—to access their innate truth and, in many cases, organize it into a new and personal mission.

The Irrevocable Happiness Exercise is quite practical in getting people to become very specific about the role, lifestyle, work, personal life, and platform that will support their highest fulfillment and joy. The exercise casts a wide net, and it can also be returned to over and over to update and refine the definitions over time.

Similarly, when we do organizational Socratic work, we ask the most open-ended questions possible and facilitate the broadest exercises in order to get our clients to become fully creative with their answers. For example, rather than limiting question, a broad question such as "How do you feel about your culture?" gives the recipient the signal to tell us anything on their mind. Wide open questions inspire conversation. They open up new and unexpected doors. If we want a more narrow focus, we can always tailor our questions. For example, we could ask, "What are some of the specific challenges with your culture?" We use less open-ended questions to define issues such as skill deficits, support requirements, performance improvements, and getting the best use out of our time. But the only reason to use closed questions, of the yes or no variety, is to stop the conversation. In fact, the only good use of a close-ended question is to politely regain control of a conversation.

One of the great strengths we can build into any organization is the ability to ask effective questions, the ones that inspire stakeholders to tell us what they want and need, the questions that get our customers to freely disclose what fulfilled expectations mean to them, and the questions that can inspire our colleagues to become receptive to our support. Here are a few examples:

- What would you like to accomplish in our meeting today?
- What is it about my leadership style that could be improved?
- How do you want to grow at our company? What kinds of skills do you need in order to do that?
- Imagine we are having lunch two years from now and you are telling me that today's discussion represented a turning point in your career. What happened?

In addition, skilled questioning improves sales, peer-to-peer innovation, leadership development, career development, customer retention, and productivity. Great questioning skills facilitate getting to the truth. And today, succeeding in the midst of rapid change requires that we get to the truth more quickly than ever before.

When an intact team comes through our program, we don't want to just sustain engagement; we want to deepen it significantly. Answering a few questions for even five minutes can not only support the development of long-term engagement, but can help employees get the most out of their day today. Here are some examples:

- What do you most want to accomplish today?
- In order to do it, what help do you need?
- What is today's ideal blend of tactical and strategic work?
- Which stakeholder(s) need your attention?
- How can you further your mission, vision, and purpose today?
- How can you best take care of yourself today?
- What would represent a big win for you today?
- Who most deserves your praise today?

Five minutes—this is all that it takes to become more centered, productive, mindful, and clear thinking. However, caution is also in order. As with all forms of communication, questions can be skewed to manipulate people and create disconnectedness. Here are some examples:

- Do you want a million dollars?

- Do you want to be more successful?

- Do you want your coworkers to like you?

Salespeople and managers who ask questions with one-answer responses possess a kind of cynicism that humans can be hypnotized into saying yes when it is time to sell their product or service. Great Socratic questions, on the other hand, capture a person's mind, critical thinking, emotional makeup, and above all, their truth. Their truth brings them back to mission, vision, and purpose. The value of investing in these great questions is that in doing so, we can galvanize our people around infinite causes. We can help them envision where they are headed, what they need to learn to stay competitive, how to better connect with colleagues, and how to "move mountains" that are important to them.

Teaching everyone the value of active listening skills is also essential to strong engagement. Why? When we ask someone an open-ended question that pertains to the circumstances at hand, the interaction compels them to listen, to think, to respond, and to open up. It helps them to better understand their colleagues. This is why we want to teach everyone these consultative sales skills. When our employees learn how to ask great questions, they become more connected to their stakeholders and also to each other. When we can connect with others' individual visions, we can then move more easily into building a shared vision. The strategic use of mentors will also play a crucial role in helping employees build a meaningful and compelling vision within their own lives as well as the shared vision within intact teams and organizations. It all works together.

Many will need to be led into this work from different beliefs they currently hold. Some, for example, will have long since given up on the idea of a personal vision. Some will have forgotten what it feels like to dream of their best life. Others will have been conditioned to run from any form of vision that leads to the need for personal change, especially because the need to change often carries a negative connotation. And yet many will respond immediately, grateful to be given the time, space, voice, and process to define what is important to them in their professional lives. Many will immediately translate this into all they want to contribute within your organization. This is a classic win-win.

I unknowingly began my love affair with Socratic work in my 20s through the sales profession. As some of you will recall, in the 1980s, many of us at the time used copiers. But, we didn't say, "Make me a copy." We said, "Make me a Xerox." The Xerox Corporation had a monopoly on photocopying until our country relaxed trade tariffs. Then, suddenly, businesses were inundated with photocopy machines from all over the world. Many offered new features and others were shockingly less expensive. The change represented the single biggest crisis in the history of Xerox. In response, the company built a sales institute to study the psychology of selling and invented a new form of business development.

Eventually Xerox opened new sales training to outsiders, and my company at the time sent me to learn and evaluate these new sales techniques for our industry. The psychologists that Xerox hired came up with a statement that drove all of my sales philosophy from that date forward. They said, "Human beings are capable of thinking of something other than themselves for a maximum of fifteen seconds." This one insight turned my outlook on sales completely on its head. It effectively rendered our standard pitch selling completely irrelevant. People don't care about your resume. They don't care about the chemical makeup of your cleaning supplies. They care about one thing and that is their own fulfilled expectations.

When I came back from the training, I immediately started teaching our sales people how to develop expertise in finding the unfulfilled needs and expectations of everyone in our market. Prior to that, we had more than 200 competitors, with sales people pouring into the streets of Los Angeles every single day. They made pitches. They overcame objections. They built relationships through sheer persistence and having a "winning personality." It was dreadfully stressful work. It also lacked soul. It was a means to an end, period.

After this discovery of a whole new approach, we sent our sales professionals into the field armed with Socratic sales questions. We asked questions that helped our prospects define for themselves how to do a better job. Our business soared. As importantly, we became more likeable. One of my clients told me, "You have the most charismatic sales people in the world." I responded, "Isn't it because they pay better attention to you than most anyone else?" She indicated that this was exactly the reason.

For many years Tom Drucker, one of the country's foremost management consultants, led Xerox Learning. We have become good friends during the past 10 years and regularly visit to trade stories and share trends. I treasure Tom for his well-developed wisdom. He lives on the beach just 6 miles south of my beach. His wife, Marcia, is an equally successful theatrical producer. I visited with Tom to discuss Socratic thought as a cultural foundation for work engagement and productivity.

> **David:** For me, what happened at Xerox represented a watershed change in how we sell products and services. Socratic-driven conversation became a far more sustainable way to influence the world. How would you describe your own learning process after Xerox?

> **Tom:** Shortly after leaving, I met Peter Senge at Esalen. We became fast friends. Peter had not yet written *The 5th Discipline*. The notion of a learning organization—in other words, an organization that facilitates the learning of its members and continuously transforms itself—was very exciting to me. One of my responsibilities had been running the Xerox Learning Center, where we taught people how to ask questions and lead dialogue. In building a learning organization, this type of Socratic inquiry, connected to a collective...produces some of our most significant culture changes.

> **David:** It sounds as if you blew Socratic inquiry wide open.

> **Tom:** Absolutely. In addition to Peter, I was heavily influenced by Marilyn Ferguson, the author of *The Brain Revolution: The Frontiers of Mind Research* (Taplinger). Her studies brought science and research into human development where learning and behavioral change actually rewires our brains. Now, we could tie the benefits of our work to science.

David: You also became heavily involved with the Word Café, the international organization devoted to question-driven learning forums. How did that impact your outlook?

Tom: The purpose of a question-driven dialogue at Xerox was the sale or getting to know the customer. Here, there was no purpose to the dialogue except what *emerged* from the dialogue; we weren't managing or pre-ordaining what we would find. This kind of interaction provides a lot more freedom for everyone else in how they responded. That freedom revealed unexpected insights into what we didn't know.

In the Word Café, we ask questions and apply no controls over the answers. We often move from one participant to the next so that everyone has the opportunity to engage in the conversation and the questions at hand.

David: How can this technique apply to engagement?

Tom: The wisdom emerges from the collective; you dig into topics. The learning is in the foreground. The process? People love it. You can extract such fabulous outcomes. I always timed these events so that feedback could be returned immediately. There is nothing more disrespectful than to ask people to participate in a communications process and then exclude them from the feedback. Here, they see the information from others and they also see their contributions are appreciated as well. The power of this type of process is you can invite customers, employees, leaders, vendors, all type of participants into the learning process. It is a great tool for overcoming isolation.

David: Many business authors and leading management consultants have talked about the need for personalized mission, vision, and purpose, but in practice it rarely happens.

Tom: It is critical for strong culture development and it is a matter of respect. No matter the environment, we need to find ways for every stakeholder to define what it is that they want out of their work, beyond the money. I was working with one organization where the ethos was all about the money and it was filled with young financial wizards. I asked them to go home and write out what they wanted beyond the income. What did they want to do with that income? What kind of lives did they want to lead? Many wanted the ability to marry and raise children. They began talking about a richness of life that was more connected to their spiritual and emotional well-being. Their answers changed the culture. We were able to introduce a 401K and use that as a platform for discussing their future.

David: I know that you are working with several organizations that have large Millennial populations. It seems we have built a new consulting industry around generational differences, and it is complicating the conversation. Baby Boomers put down the Millennials as self-involved and irresponsible. In the end, it is simply about fighting for turf. Rather than talking about differences, what does everyone want and need?

Tom: I am so in accord with this. First, everyone wants to be treated as we want others to treat us.

There are studies that show Millennials are job hoppers. They are not. They want to be appreciated. They don't need "atta boy" or "atta girl." They want to be appreciated for their thoughts and ideas. The reason they leave jobs is their superiors often don't see them as collaborative and fully formed adults. They treat them as children, as fungible units. They don't take them into confidences.

People need to be mentored. They need to be included. If they don't live up to standards, they need to be taught how to behave. They want to be successful. They don't want to come all this way and fail. They want adult bonds. They want an adult-to-adult relationship. When they feel that, they blossom. People thrive when they are connected. This is all about emotional intelligence and rather than complicating the narrative with differences; it is so important that we always remember the Golden (or even "platinum") Rule.

David: You are working on an ambitious project to transform the culture, customer service, and talent strategies for VCA, the country's largest veterinarian group.

Tom: They are devoted to building the finest customer and pet care experience in the industry, and with 25,000 employees, it is a very large project.

David: Where did you begin?

Tom: We begin with emotional intelligence. Yes, many of the customer-care and back-room areas are populated with young people who join the business because of their love for animals. The longer-term employees have found ways to take care of themselves through the extremes. The environment includes people coming in to let go of their companions with all the heartbreak that implies, and others coming in with the joyful rituals from having new pets. Their day includes difficult customers rattled with their dog's health issues. We have the shock of critical injuries.

We cannot expect employees to be their best if we don't create the kinds of rituals and care that emotionally nourishes them. For example, we have a daily ritual that everyone uses called "the huddle." One takes place in the front office, another in the back, and one with the vets. We gather together and check in with each member of the team with questions like, "How are you doing? You had the flu last week. How are you holding up?" "Jennifer, you sat with that lady early this morning who was too distraught to get up. You were so kind to her. How can we support you?" "Paul, what you did with that irate customer was awesome! How did you come up with that?"

These ritualized bonds and conversations help nourish people to be their best. We can provide all of the techniques in the world but without watching each other's back, being appreciative and kind, we will not get their best.

David: If you are meeting with a CEO with significant cynicism and contempt around talent development and employer branding, how do you work with them?

Tom: Well, first you acknowledge them for taking the meeting and even being willing to explore the questions. Usually, I suggest that we start with a small project or pilot program, an opportunity for "proof of concept." The results will speak for themselves. In reality, CEOs and business owners who understand the truth about talent and the Golden Rule are not the norm. I had the great privilege of working for David Kearns at Xerox. He was one of those rare individuals who always did the right thing. Very much like your friend at the U.S. Marines, he led the company with values, he paid attention to the employees, and he treated everyone with dignity. He expected others to do the same. Other large companies were pouring poison into the river or cheating communities out of water. Many treated their employees like numbers. It feels so right but after moving on, I realized just how unusual it is to have a CEO who embraces those standards all of the time.

Where do we now take the power of the Socratic process? It's very simple. Start using the questions. Teach everyone to start using questions to access truth whether it is in a sales setting, personal career development journaling, connecting with stakeholders, or leading an organization through difficult change. There is a series of sample questions at the conclusion of *The Workplace Engagement Solution*. Better yet, develop a Socratic Question Library within your own organization and encourage employees to send in their best questions and the memorable breakthroughs they have had in helping each other live in the truth. The truth, after all, is what we need most in a world of rapidly accelerating change. Perhaps it is what we needed all along. Instead of living with a "barrenness of life," we can develop richly flourishing lives filled with the kind of meaning and purpose that promotes enthusiasm and energy.

5

The Visibility Initiative

Envision an environment filled with workers who pursue rather than run from change, one in which workers change their outlooks and connect with themselves, the people around them, and their customers. Imagine that, as a result, you are better able to grow their careers as well as your organization's future. In this mentor-driven and truly democratic culture, it is pervasive gratitude, the single greatest fuel for high morale and performance, that has become the signature of your workplace.

The wise holocaust survivor and philosopher Elie Wiesel said, "When a person doesn't have gratitude, something is missing in his or her humanity. A person can almost be defined by his or her attitude toward gratitude."[1] This dynamic that Mr. Wiesel describes can exponentially grow in its impact on an organization. Over the years, I have often been asked to help an employer decide between two top candidates. I usually respond, "Hire the one that is most grateful." Why? These are the individuals that are inherently skilled in connecting with others; they bring positive energy to a team, and they demonstrate predictably strong and sustained performance.

Building the skills of engagement and the capacity to change requires that we learn how to become comfortable and skilled in connecting with others in a wide variety of circumstances. Every single day, organizations in America spend about half a billion dollars on training. The value of this training is often diminished by the fact that giving one skills training session is rarely enough to change long-term behavior. In contrast, the skill building suggested in *The Workplace Engagement Solution* isn't complicated, yet the long-term sustainability is guaranteed by marrying the suggested skill improvements to smart mentorship. Mentorship, when used consistently and broadly, provides the continuity that makes valuable behavioral changes a permanent part of the culture.

We work towards building organizations filled with talented people who can also connect, look people in the eye, ask skilled questions, and demonstrate active listening. We seek to grow talent that explores the world of change around them, defines needed change within themselves, and speaks the truth. And as our talent develops the skills that build strong support systems, new intelligence flows in from the outside world, bringing innovation and critical improvements to organizational performance. As they build stronger relationships within and without, the culture becomes unstoppable. Employees develop an unparalleled sense of gratitude that stems from their ongoing personal growth, the precious quality of their work relationships, and the unshakable confidence that they can deal with anything the world of change dishes out to them. Yes, the reality will be messier than this bold vision suggests, but it is where we set our intentions that is so very important. And why shouldn't we aspire to this?

Let's start with the skills of drawing healthy attention to ourselves and, conversely, in giving high quality attention to others. Take a moment to think through this notion. With any customer contact role, learning how to draw healthy attention to ourselves and also to give that to others can never be over-applied. In fact, developing these skills within everyone is nothing short of transformative. How do we do this? We teach them the new skills and then we mentor them into sustained behavioral improvements. I call this the "Visibility Initiative" and it includes three specific skill development programs.

Connecting (Sales Training)

Good salespeople are masterful at connecting with others. They listen more actively and effectively. They methodically ask stakeholders the questions that uncover their needs and expectations. They are more aware of other people's body language and tone of voice. Good salespeople put themselves into the mindset of giving and creating value. Skilled selling helps us to discover what makes people tick. It tends to connect us with passion and this makes us more effective in selling ideas, concepts, and innovations. This is the exact opposite of disengagement. In fact, it's full engagement. It is a pervasive energy that awakens the team and larger environment. This is one of the many reasons why everyone benefits from sales training.

An across-the-board, inclusive mentoring practice is also critical. When we build strong mentors, it isn't necessary to send employees to extensive and expensive training programs. If we give our people particularly effective, brief, yet profound learning opportunities followed by consistent mentorship, no time is wasted and the embedded day-to-day support ensures that the new skills translate into lasting behavioral changes.

The experience of selling can be very uncomfortable at first. Yet with consistent exposure and practice, it builds confidence and helps people become more comfortable in drawing attention to themselves as well as connecting with others. Sales training provides options and can increase income. Learning how to sell can even help someone move beyond their past.

When I joined the staffing industry at 24, I was afraid of my own shadow. I grew up in an abusive household and attention, for me, produced almost-violent responses. I stuttered. I often trembled. My voice quavered. All this meant that learning to be good at selling at my new job was a big challenge, but in my head I believed that I had to stick with it if I was going to survive. Within months, I was making good money while also becoming more confident in every other aspect of my life. My career choices forced me into visibility. That journey changed who I became. And I have watched visibility change thousands of other people's lives as well.

I encourage selecting training programs that are consultative and question-driven versus solely pitch-driven. The world of making a pitch and overcoming objections is one of the reasons many people are frightened of selling. They have good reason to be. It is not a high integrity and satisfying method for engaging and influencing people. It rarely adds to the meaningfulness of our sales interactions or work. In our training programs, we find that many participants actually become enthusiasts when they realize that consultative selling is essentially good communications. It is the kind of human interaction that puts the buyer at ease. It leads to quality relationships.

Speaking Up (Presentation Skills Training)

As we continue, it is important to remember that the context for this conversation is about helping people get past the barriers they have in connecting with others. The skills of connecting are also the skills needed to gracefully move through change. Creating an environment that builds good presentation skills offers opportunities for people to present what is valuable to them. It opens doors to stronger career paths. It inspires colleagues to become more supportive of one another. It creates an environment that applauds the positive aspects within every employee. Strong presentation skills will create new brand ambassadors who are capable of articulating the multi-dimensional benefits of becoming a customer or an employee with your organization. The experience of becoming a better presenter also helps people become more comfortable in their own skin.

This kind of cultural mojo is not only attractive within the organization, but is magnetic to the outside world. Even better, building this skill set produces more resilience during difficult times. I have often witnessed the strong bonds that grow from a broadly inclusive presentation skills initiative, and these are the very bonds that can help valued talent stay when the chips are down. What an asset for any organization.

A few things are important when providing your employees with presentation skills training. For example, it ought to include actual presentations in front of a room, on camera, and via virtual platforms. The attributes of the program need to provide understanding around body language, posture, tone of voice, and content development. Many of us are clueless that human beings, for thousands of years, functioned without words. We relied on tone of voice, facial expressions, and body language for communication. Even today, most communication studies find that we respond more strongly to these three characteristics than the words coming out of our mouths. As a musician, I pay more attention to the music in people's voices than the actual words. Many of us who want to connect more effectively have never paid attention to these traits because no one ever told us of their value. Consider the impact from improving our tone of voice, body language, and facial expressions into communication skills that help employees connect more effectively with each other, customers, and the outside world. Consider what will happen when our colleagues become more confident with presentation skills and start speaking up with ideas, innovation, and new value.

The importance of online presentation skills will only grow in the future. Right now, many organizations are building production studios to support most business development and client development meetings. It saves time and money. Developing the skills to be effective in these mediums will improve every aspect of performance and profit. Emerging technology behind virtual reality will also continue to transform training, business development, and employee meetings in ways that will require even more advanced skills in this area. For those who continue to resist change, who are perhaps still complaining about using social networking platforms that emerged 10 years ago, beware the dinosaur syndrome.

But rather than getting caught up with the changes ahead, the point of providing presentation skills training for all employees is especially about their abilities to connect, listen, organize thoughts, appreciate others, and generally build consistency within the culture as well as bench strength for the entire organization. Building and deepening these skills also requires continuity, which can take place in casual "lunch and learn" sessions in which employees can take turns presenting to each other. It is also easy and inexpensive to establish a Toastmasters chapter within your organization. All that you need are 20 people over the age of 18. If your business isn't large enough, there are invariably Toastmasters Chapters nearby as well.

Long before organizations started seeing the value of across-the-board presentation training, Dale Carnegie touted the benefits to everyone who would listen. In his book *The Art of Public Speaking*, he said:

> Students of public speaking continually ask, "How can I overcome self-consciousness and the fear that paralyzes me before an audience?" Did you ever notice in looking from a train window that some horses feed near the track and never even pause to look up at the thundering cars, while just ahead at the next railroad crossing a farmer's wife will be nervously trying to quiet her scared horse as the train goes by? How would you cure a horse that is afraid of cars—graze him in a back-woods lot where he would never see steam-engines or automobiles? Or would you drive or pasture him where he would frequently experience the noise and commotion accompanying the machines?[2]

Mr. Carnegie's point of view is so pure and simple, and yet it applies directly to what I am advocating here. For those of us who find connecting with people to be painful, jumping in, plunging into the water changes the game. Learning to stand in front of our peers will lead us to stop shying away from opportunities to connect. Without doing it, we can read about the subject for years and never attain any progress.

Beyond the fear are also some beautiful gifts. Plunging in together can be a very exciting, celebrative, and deeply bonding experience. All the while, the immersion into this new territory gives us an understanding of how to connect with the world around us in new and meaningful ways. And so I say, it's time to speak up!

Community Building (Social Networking)

Gary Vaynerchuk wisely said, "When I hear people debate the ROI of social media it reminds me why so many businesses fail. Most businesses are not playing the marathon. They're playing the sprint. They're not worried about a lifetime value and retention. They're worried about short-term goals."[3]

I am continually surprised at the marginal competency most people have with using social media to build their careers, their businesses, and, more importantly, their communities. We can witness the marginal value social networking has in the workplace through the debates about its appropriateness and clumsy policies around social media use among employees. As they fumble around, social media is currently the fastest, most effective medium for growing a successful support system. Motivational speaker Jim Rohn famously said, "You are the average of the five people you spend the most time with."[4] We can recast this statement today by suggesting that your social media success is based on the average of the five thousand people in your network. Social media is where we live today.

My advocacy for universal social media skills came from a deeply personal experience. I characterize October 2008 as the business owner's 9/11. Most of my entrepreneurial friends can recount where they were and what they were doing when they found out the economy was collapsing. My own company lost about a third of our contracts during the first week and the balance were gone by the end of the first month. We had a gentleman who sat in his office for hours working on business development with LinkedIn. After a year, the results were so minimal that I used that experience to support my own cynicism about investing in social media. My business development success up until that time had been based on proven formulas such as making sales calls, building face-to-face persistent sales skills, and engaging in lots of follow-up, lunches, personalized notes, and regular calls. All of a sudden, I had very little to show for it.

Out of some desperation and growing curiosity, I took a much closer look at social networking and realized that most of us were experiencing something like the following.

We receive a generic, automated note that says "I would like to add you to my connections." We often wonder what they want and mostly feel they are likely trying to sell to us. We mindlessly accept the connection. We may briefly glance at their profile. We never hear from them again.

As a technical platform, social networking offers speed and access in ways that humble old sales skills such as prospecting, qualifying, knocking on doors, and getting in do not. The core problem with typical social networking competency is that the vast majority of it resembles junk mail and inserts very little warmth, attractiveness, and connectivity in our approach. So I designed a high-touch business development protocol into social networking, and the results were staggering. At the time I had maybe 400 connections that primarily included people that I already knew or people that I had never talked with. Today I have more than 11,000 connections, most of them active and more than 90 percent of them are people that I had never met or talked to previously. Today, *most* of our new business comes from social networking with referrals as a close second. I used social networking to build my publishing platform. My blogs now reach more than six million readers.

So much time is spent on studying generational differences and what to do about the Millennials; we actually have so much to learn from their success with social media. On *60 Minutes*, Bill Whitaker asked Kim Kardashian, "Other people sing, or they do comedy. What's your talent?"

> **Kim:** "It is a talent to create a brand that is really successful off of getting people to like you for you."
>
> **Whitaker:** "You've turned you into an empire, worth in excess of a $100 million dollars, I've read."
>
> **Kim:** "I would think that involves some kind of talent."[5]

Taylor Swift is the world's master of building profoundly connected relationships with her fans through the savvy use of social media. Swift is part of a generation that used social media throughout their developmental years. What makes Taylor Swift so unique within the industry is that she builds these relationships not by touting her glory but by giving high-quality attention to her fans, asking them to share their needs and wants, their joys, fears, and dreams. They become part of a narrative that tightly bonds them to the star. Her social media practices are not only brilliant, her skills represent the types that I promote: high touch, engaging, and focused on the fans rather than on oneself. CEOs and marketing executives would do well to study her marketing genius. What does this have to do with employee engagement and personal change?

We want to not only promote social networking within our organizations, we want to give people the kinds of skills that help them rapidly connect with the people that can contribute to their personal and professional growth. For the last three years, we have taken the social networking process I created to rebuild Inspired Work and turned it into a social networking curriculum that is delivered to intact teams and professionals, both in classroom and virtual environments. We teach people how to define an online brand with their profile and their communications. The brand is designed to provide consistency and attractiveness. More importantly, we teach people to never rely on generic site-based communications ever again. We show people how to reach out to prospective connections with messages that are about them rather than about us. The communication progression begins with comfortable and casual dialogue, and mindfully builds the relationship to the point of a phone call or face-to-face meeting. For the more ambitious, the final training module gets them started with online publishing, blogging, and style differences across a broad series of platforms such as Twitter and Facebook.

The benefits of building social networking skills are endless. Human resources departments use social media to strengthen recruitment efforts while lowering costs. They quickly and easily establish new sources of business intelligence. They build relationships with other human resources organizations. They develop stronger careers by locating skilled mentors. Financial professionals stay abreast of innovation and trends. Others realize they actually love this form of community building and become skilled bloggers themselves.

But let us return to the steps involved in successful personal change. The obstacle "they'll hurt me" accompanies drawing healthy attention to oneself. For the vast number of individuals who work very hard to avoid attention, this process can be life-changing. Simply pointing out the obstacle creates awareness and begins to remove some of the blind spots that lead to hiding in one's own skin. Developing the actual skills can impact every aspect of organizational performance while transforming confidence levels. When we also add mentorship and peer forums to further develop the skills, we observe a new level of appreciation and awareness for one another.

Why do I consistently add the word "healthy" to attention? Organizations will generally have a number of employees who grew up in environments filled with negative attention. Biologically, the human nervous system requires attention to function in a healthy way. At the core, our nervous system doesn't differentiate between good and bad attention. Consequently, those of us who grew up in negative circumstances will often find ways to get attention through negativity. These are the individuals who often create disruption during change and confront colleagues in inappropriate ways. Many of them are also significant contributors and revenue generators, so we put up with them. But as we develop healthy attention-getting skills within our talent, we provide opportunities to mentor and coach these valued team members so that they gain insight about how they are operating and what they can do to improve going forward.

This whole area of getting attention reveals the best and the worst in us. Some individuals may have such deep-seated negative behavior— or perhaps they simply don't fit within the culture—that it will become clear that it is time to part ways. This is a good outcome. After taking all the necessary steps to turn a situation around, departure is not a loss; it is an improvement. For example, when we take intact teams through the Inspired Work Program, about 5 percent will self-select to leave within 30 days and 2 percent will be counseled out. Invariably, these are the individuals who are routinely discussed in briefings with our internal partners, taking up valuable time and energy. The partner may make statements such as "I don't know if he is working out" or "She does nothing but attack progress and new ideas." Countless managers are surprised by the comments and behaviors that emerge from employees who work in highly siloed environments after participating in our program. In essence, these developmental turning points give everyone the opportunity to examine where they are with attention, engagement, connectivity, and enthusiasm for growth. The process is transformative and improves the circumstances of establishing responsibility for all behavior.

Throughout the development process, leaders can contribute to raising the value of the outcomes by establishing their expectations for engagement, change, connecting with others, and building one's confidence. Mentors should be briefed on desired improvements with team members. But this is often not even necessary. We find that when people go through the self-inquiry process, we are proposing they are far more willing to take the initiative to change, to develop their courage, and to ask for support. This is actually a healthier dynamic, one in which individual employees take full ownership of their own career success. But it is important to know that you should only promote sales, presentation, and networking skills to your people after they have engaged in self-inquiry exercises and found their internal motivation. Without this, developing talent can be exhausting and ineffective for all involved.

Throughout the process of developing these skills, it is important to teach the value of giving and also accepting praise. It is a time to praise employees who demonstrate courage. Those who step forward with significant fear of presenting, who not only live through the experience but consequently have a breakthrough, are the ones we most want to acknowledge and reward. They will become the most potent role models for those who are still frightened by the process of building these skills. So let your "rock stars" shine!

Compassion is also a key ingredient in making the experience as illuminating as possible. When giving feedback about presentations, about anything that requires courage, the last thing we want to do is give hurtful messaging. Award them for the courage it took to stand-up. If they are clearly afraid, save any critiques for later. Praise them again and then suggest ways that future presentations can be more effective. In the spirit of building a high-quality, healthy-attention environment, promote the practice of not taking anything personally. It is through the practice of not taking anything personally that everyone becomes more of a partner in learning how to connect at the highest levels.

The visibility initiative offers organizations an opportunity to create a strong and healthy relationship with the outside world, a richly rewarding interior world, and an environment that fosters unexpected growth. Some will question it, but many others will come to see the value despite their initial discomfort. You will also have brave pioneers who will plunge in easily and emerge with deep gratitude. These are your mentors.

6

The Support System

Many people don't pursue what they really want because, at their core, they believe they will never get the help that would bring their vision to life. Once we define a mission, vision, and purpose, however, our success is purely based on the quality of help we get from others. The most successful people in the world either intuitively or consciously understand that if they are going to realize their dreams and ambitions, they must get the right people to help them. For example, when a long-term executive decides to start their own business, an entirely new support system is in order. Mentors, teachers, coaches, vendors, and administrative, business development and financial support all come into play when someone makes such a big life change. Those who don't understand this fact of life are basically walling themselves off from their best and highest usefulness. In the modern world, those of us who believe we must do it all on our own often find ourselves running in circles and chasing our tails. Support and collaboration are key success drivers in our increasingly complex world.

The concept of building success through building meaningful support systems is so elusive that we sometimes mindlessly put down the process in front of our children. For example, the Emmy, Academy, and Grammy Awards represent an extraordinary opportunity for us to point out how the most successful people in media made it to those podiums. However, we complain as the award winners go on and on thanking all the people who helped them by generously giving their time, putting their necks on the line, and otherwise investing blood, sweat, and tears into the success at hand. Many of us assume they bought that support system once they became rich and famous rather than pointing out to our children they became rich and famous because of that support system. Large swaths of talented people aren't engaged, don't change, and become paralyzed with fear because they don't have a reliable support system and don't have the skills to build one.

When I began the Inspired Work journey, doing everything myself was the norm. Designing work solutions for others brought the unexpected reward of ending my lifelong experience of pushing an egg up a hill with my nose. How ironic, right? The purpose of this first program was to "[i]nstill an awareness of the work we were born to do and recognize the skill sets that bring the vision to life. We don't abide by the standards of average; we stand with Irrevocable Happiness."

I finished the first two-thirds of the curriculum in less than a week. Bringing people to personalized visions came naturally to me. Then, I ran into a brick wall. At the time, my natural inclination to bring a vision to life, to make it a practical reality, was simply to work harder. Without a mindset intervention, this was my natural pattern. My adoptive father was a Russian immigrant who had worked in a labor camp where the community had a favorite saying: "Work tastes better than food." He became a medical doctor. As a former concert pianist, I worked in practice studios for so many hours that I often had blood coming from the edges of my fingernails. In our Inspired Work programs, that magic moment arrives when someone announces a breakthrough, a new career, a new business, or a commitment to learning new behavior. I ask the question, "What are you going to do now?" The response is usually some form of "work harder." When we come from that mindset, at best we are going to burn out, but usually we will simply fail.

I was climbing the walls looking for answers about how to complete the curriculum. The Academy Awards show was on television. *Driving Miss Daisy*, Jessica Tandy, and Oliver Stone were having quite the night, with newcomer Daniel-Day Lewis grabbing an award for *My Left Foot*.[1] Suddenly, it hit me:

- Everything of value in this world is done through collaboration.
- We can live in the delusion that we don't need support for many years.
- If we are going to succeed with any form of a unique career path, our success can only be derived from getting others to help us.
- Perhaps best of all, people *want* to help.

This was a turning point that got passed on to thousands of our participants. Not only do many of us have inadequate support in our careers, we can also extend that deficiency to our healthcare, love lives, finances, social standing, image, childcare, personal development, and continuous education. From the lens of inadequate support, we live with problems that seem to have no solution. We work harder to get past them, but we don't get anywhere. Or, we get there while other vital aspects of our lives suffer. This is no optimal way to live.

The entire learning and development field works to help organizations provide their talent with certain forms of growth support, but how many spend time teaching their people how to acquire the right forms of support? It seems a bit counterintuitive that to become self-sufficient, we must learn how to identify, recruit, and manage help from others, doesn't it? And yet, that is exactly how success works.

Our critical thinking mind would probably accept these views as basic common sense, yet we have been conditioned from the current work world to view requests for help with a variety of strange, unhealthy, yet relatively common beliefs such as:

- If I ask for help, people will think that I don't know what I'm doing.
- If I want something done right, I have to do it myself.
- There is something wrong with asking for help.
- What will people think if I ask for help and how will they talk about it?
- No one will want to help me.

This is not the inner dialogue of successful people, nor are these sentiments common in our highest-performing organizations. In fact, our most successful entrepreneurs, CEOs, political leaders, and media figures surround themselves with the smartest advisors, mentors, and teachers. It is part of their success equation.

During the Inspired Work program, we help people define and craft a mission that is so personally compelling that they become invested in doing whatever it takes to make it happen. We also guide them into the crucial awareness that all will come together, in part, by assembling the right help.

How do we bring the right kind of help into an organization? How do we create a model that isn't paternalistic, doesn't break the bank, is self-sustaining, and grows over time? We do it by building a transformative mentor-based culture.

The Mentor-Based Culture

The world's most successful leadership development organization is the United States Marine Corps. The world's most effective mentoring organization is Alcoholics Anonymous (AA). There is great value in studying why the constructs of these organizations work so well and are so effective.

The Marines are highly successful in leadership development because they practice and live by values on a day-to-day basis. AA also succeeds through the continuous practice of values, however it is their mentorship model that bears much closer examination. AA is the world's largest recovery "organization" and yet it has no formal infrastructure. It doesn't market. There are no dues or fees. It began with two individuals and now has an estimated membership of more than two million alcoholics and drug addicts around the world. Throughout the AA community, you will find countless individuals with years or even decades of sobriety. AA's effectiveness is based on values and mentorship. Mentors are those who learn how to use the program and provide the committed guidance that most human beings require in order to achieve long-term behavioral change. The mentors are not paid, yet they are attracted to become mentors because it deepens their own member skills and helps them to stay engaged. They experience great rewards by watching others flourish and thrive with their support. These are characteristics that many organizations should strive to achieve.

We apply these examples by creating a mentor-based culture that takes the early adopters of the skills, principals, values, and practices outlined in this book and encouraging them to become mentors to others. The mentors will help others grow the skills of change and engagement. They remind others to engage in regular self-inquiry and help their fellow colleagues deal with blind spots and old behaviors that need to be replaced. They help their colleagues find the right learning resources and support systems for their particular areas of growth. Mentors support and encourage their colleagues while they continue meeting the responsibilities of their own work. They manage their time effectively.

Mentors also celebrate progress at every turn. They become even more successful themselves because they are taking their own learning and growth to an entirely new level. They become valued allies. As the mentor base grows, the foundation and bench strength of the entire organization transforms. As a result of building this mentor-based model of working, overall productivity, morale, and engagement increase, developing a culture of excellence and caring.

When we build a mentor-driven culture, we establish an entirely new form of organizational performance by orchestrating the expansion of everyone's abilities to change and engage. It will inevitably lower turnover and establish a true democratic environment in which anyone with initiative can build life-changing skills and help others to do the same. People want to work in environments like these.

The Mentor

Mentors have one of the most honored roles in our society. They have reached success and have a generosity for helping others do the same. The payoffs in becoming someone's mentor include special recognition and a deepening of the skills they also find so valuable. But, there is another, even more precious, payoff.

One of the erroneous beliefs in our culture is that service isn't valuable unless it is selfless. Nothing could be further from the truth.

Service to others changes our sense of self-worth and chips away at negative views about ourselves we too often dwell on. When we practice service, there comes a time when we look in the mirror and are more proud and happy about the person we have become.

In a democracy, everyone engages in the agreed-upon practice. Mentors are the ones who adopt that practice first and successfully. They are also the ones who support long-term behavioral change. These mentors will then become one of the most valued assets in producing robust engagement, strong talent development, and enthusiasm throughout the culture.

At certain points in this narrative, I will be using words such as "mentor," "teacher," and "coach." The differences are quite simple:

- A mentor is contributing his or her experience, skills, and influence as a gift. In other words, they are giving their time. The reward is that it helps their continued growth.

- A coach does much the same but sends a bill.

- A teacher provides learning experiences, usually around specific topics.

Mentors have the capacity to support others without setting aside their core professional responsibilities. In other words, they manage their time effectively and continually work on their capacity to produce progress and accountability in others.

Here are the overall characteristics of a strong mentor:

- Supports the development of engagement and change skills in their mentees.

- Actively engages him or herself.

- Develops the skills of personal change.

- Quickly sets aside cynicism, contempt, aimlessness, resignation, and frenzy, and helps others do the same.

- Continuously engages mentors to support his or her own personal growth.

- Develops the discipline and balance of meeting their core work responsibilities as they also support others.

- Is a champion for others in personal growth, change, and engagement.
- Gently leads their colleagues into continuous growth and education.

But what do they actually teach? What do they do and remind others to do?

Self-Inquiry

Periodically, a mentor will ask his or her colleague to engage in an in-depth self-inquiry exercise regarding career fulfillment, as well as to update their personal mission, vision, and purpose. Self-inquiry will then be tied to new educational needs and any necessary adjustments to their support system.

Mentors will periodically observe their assigned colleagues are disengaging or falling behind in development. When this happens, they will ask their mentee to engage in the appropriate self-inquiry exercises or connect with the right support systems. In some cases, simply providing support to that individual will help them "snap out of it."

Skill-Building

A good mentor evaluates where their mentee stands with respect to overall skill-building needs. For some, aspects of skill-building will bring out fear and discomfort. This is normal, but can be managed in the conversation. The mentor will encourage and inspire their colleagues to move forward, often by sharing their own stories in how they overcame their fear, embraced change, and succeeded in the learning process. Mentors will discuss learning options and keep them in a growth process. The endgame will be in producing successful colleagues with strong skills in sales, presentations, social networking, and building effective support systems.

The Support System

For many, building an extensive support system will represent a new territory. The mentor helps fellow employees identify and build a support system that fits their professional mission, vision, and purpose.

Together, they will discuss how to build support both internally and externally. For example, external support systems can include finding effective educational program, locating specialized healthcare resources, and finding external mentors within the industry. The mentors do none of the footwork. They guide the activities of the mentee and provide suggestions.

There is a code of conduct among the world's great mentors and teachers. They expect their students will listen, respect their input, and follow their suggestions. Period. If the mentee or student can't or won't, then it is time for them to find a new mentor or teacher. Mentors are never expected to give up their success in sacrifice to someone they are supporting. They use support to bring them greater success and satisfaction in their work. Once again, if you are getting supported from a mentor, do the things they suggest, respect their time, and reward them with praise when their support turns into gold. Sometimes the mentee and mentor relationship will not work. Just move on, and don't take it personally.

It is so important to establish this expectation throughout the organization and within the mentorship as well. Time is precious. Respect is critical to our collective success.

The Development of Courage

A good mentor or coach is effective at enticing their clients to accomplish more than they would accomplish on their own. They also know when not to push too hard. They don't want the individual to implode and understand this could cause backtracking in their progress. When we help people move beyond themselves, however, we will find their fear and discomfort. But when mentors bump into these places, they will acknowledge the fears and promote courage in the face of them. They will take a stand for establishing the willingness to take action even when frightened, and this will become a source of personal and organizational growth. At this point, the relationship with a mentor becomes even more valuable because risk-taking happens more easily when we have someone to comfort, guide, and educate us.

During the course of the last 26 years, I have learned the single greatest reason people fail is isolation. The mentor is critically important in helping others rise at these key moments where courage is needed to transcend to the next level. Perhaps their most valuable role is to remove the isolation by helping everyone connect and stand in the light. What an extraordinary opportunity this is to create a caring and supportive culture without losing the individual or collective edge.

The Praise Game

It is virtually impossible to build a strong support system without becoming skilled and generous with praise. Common sense dictates this as obvious, yet in reality, many of us are not very good at routinely recognizing the contributions of others or graciously accepting the acknowledgements that are directed towards us. We have been strongly socialized to be humble, and though being humble is honorable, it is over-applied. We all require worthy praise and it is a healthy practice we can all be better at.

One of the basic drivers of success and fulfillment is in knowing that our lives make a difference. Mentors will find that developing the skill of praising within everyone becomes one of the more pleasurable aspects of their role. Praise generates gratitude, enthusiasm, loyalty, high performance, and being focused on positive rather than negative outcomes. Praise often gets cast aside due to our general busyness as well as a fear of being visible. But when we tell those in our support systems how they made a difference in our work and in our lives, they become even more committed to supporting us.

In our social networking training, we tell our participants to not ask for professional endorsements. Instead, we advise that they give them! For example, LinkedIn provides a feature that allows us to write endorsements for people in our connections. I have developed a practice that when I am having a bad day, one of my favorite activities is to write endorsements for other people. When writing them, it is good to be genuine, specific, and generous. Not only does it lift my mood immediately, but within a few moments, the recipient is having a better day as well. When they receive and read the endorsement, LinkedIn suggests that we return the favor by writing a recommendation for the sender. Writing an endorsement in a state of gratitude often produces far better acknowledgements than when we go out and ask for them. Try it yourself and see what happens.

A few years back, I was working with a group of medical doctors who were running a surgery center. They were in a market that was fiercely competitive for nurses and their turnover with nurses was almost 40 percent per year. In evaluating the environment, it became clear that the center operated with a high level of stress from the caseload as well as the nature of the work.

Self-esteem is based on an awareness of one's productivity and worthiness. These nurses were productive, but the only time they got feedback was when they did something wrong. So we trained the physicians to praise their nurses and give them positive feedback. Turnover plummeted to 8 percent with this one easy yet powerful difference.

In a world fixated on short-term gains, we can too easily join the flurry of activity to try and meet the seemingly endless need to keep up, only to find ourselves on the proverbial hamster wheel of existence. But simple, ample praise can humanize the experience and connect us to the side of ourselves that is positive, that feels optimistic, and that grows in strength throughout our workforce. The praise game ought to be practiced at every opportunity possible. There is literally no downside.

There is also another side to praise that determines if our support system grows or falters.

As mentors praise the people they work with, it is important to pay attention to their mentees' responses. If they give some form of genuine "thank you," then simply move forward. But, what do we do if they say, "Oh, it was nothing." When we give someone a gift and they respond, "You shouldn't have," what are they actually telling us?

"Don't pay attention to me." "Don't' look at me." "I don't deserve this."

Good mentors will remind us that a simple and generous "thank you" is the response of choice. Indeed, the more generous we are with thanking someone, the more probable is they will do something nice for us again and again. Some of our great public figures have also shared their differing points-of-view about praise. Collectively, their voices are incredibly insightful:

- "The more you praise and celebrate your life, the more there is in life to celebrate." Oprah Winfrey[2]

- "The trouble with most of us is that we would rather be ruined by praise than saved by criticism." Norman Vincent Peale[3]

- "Nothing is more effective than sincere, accurate praise, and nothing is more lame than a cookie-cutter compliment." Bill Walsh[4]

The Jump Start

So how do we begin the workplace transformation? Simple. Give everyone a copy of *The Workplace Engagement Solution*. Start a book club where employees are reading and discussing its principles of change and engagement. Encourage feedback and welcome individuals who want to become early adopters to step forward and lead.

Launching an effective mentor development programs begins with selecting candidates that demonstrate a high degree of initiative, are eager to grow, and that have an optimistic outlook. In particular, pick people who will be grateful to become a part of your initiative. Get them involved in the solution's self-inquiry exercises. Have them work with each other until it becomes their natural behavior. Praise them for their efforts.

Invest in skill-building programs that hone expertise in consultative sales, presentation skills, and strategic social networking. As they realize the personal benefits of developing these "courage skills," they will be more capable of helping others do the same. The timeline for this initial development process can take place during the course of three to six months. This gives a long enough window to become really engaged in the learning process. We don't need masters of each characteristic and skill, but we do need enthusiastic buy-in and an overall understanding of what we are going to accomplish and why. Most importantly, because we are discussing a practice, we must understand that it never ends; it only grows, deepens, and broadens. It becomes a way of life.

As your mentors grow in their effectiveness, so will your culture. You'll be bringing a series of new dimensions into the workplace, and at the core will be mentors who gain the enormous personal benefits that can only be derived from uplifting others.

7

What Is an Engagement CEO?

Full and sustainable employee engagement begins with a CEO or business owner. The true "Engagement CEO" has the kind of awareness and commitment to recognize the mindset and skills required in a fully engaged organization. Much of the employee engagement "industry" tiptoes around this subject. God forbid someone loses a consulting assignment because we asked too much of the CEO! But let's be clear: this is what it takes. But what does it mean to be an Engagement CEO?

An Engagement CEO:

1. Takes charge of the culture personally.

2. Develops a strong leadership brand as evidenced in their consistent behavior and messaging.

3. Walks the talk, leads by example, and leans toward democracy over elitism in any form.

4. Expresses continuous, genuine, and worthy praise to their employees.

5. Constantly seeks ways to keep their talent current and relevant.

6. Treats employees as the organization's greatest asset versus a potential liability.

7. Packages engagement as a profit source rather than an expense.

8. Effectively manages and educates all stakeholders in the need for effective people initiatives.

9. Moves the vision from short-term financial performance to long term-value, brand strength, and reputation.

10. Tells themselves and others the truth, especially about change.

11. Keeps themselves directly connected to the front line.

12. Is transparent and expects transparency throughout their organization.

13. Shows respect towards all employees and learns from all of them.

CEOs of public companies have a specific group of stakeholders that usually need to be masterfully won over. Shareholders are often the biggest influences that push CEOs into short-term profit pushes rather than long-term growth. CEOs intent on building the business into its highest and strongest place need to link the development of people to that growth. Linking engagement to profit is one of the ways to secure their long-term support.

If any or all of these sound crazy or seem elusive to you, let's start by understanding some of the beliefs that routinely get in the way of these characteristics being more common.

"Engagement initiatives are a sidebar activity, a perk provided to our employees."

In truth, the business purpose of employee engagement is far more rigorous than simply making employees feel better. Being awake and present, journeying through change, and becoming better and more competent through the years represents one of the best and most demanding potential performance growth initiatives. Getting there demands everyone's involvement and support, including as a leader who insists on across-the-board excellence.

"It's cheaper and easier to hire new employees rather
than keep someone who is working in 'the trance.'"

In most cases, a CEO can justify high turnover to their shareholders. Minimal questions will be asked. On the other hand, they tend to give up on long-term investments such as building a category-leading workforce or developing the kind of talent that produces results that exceed all of the shareholder targets. But here is what's unrealistic about this belief. If only 13 percent of the world's workers are highly engaged, where are we going to go out and get them? Without leveraging a strong and rising employer brand, this widely held idea is delusional and also dismissive of one of the great opportunities for all businesses that is available right here and right now.

Become the greatest employer brand in your market. Develop the greatest talent pool. Create a workforce so magnetic and positive that customers come because they look forward to the experience. Build a culture so caring and supportive that people grow into their best selves. This is the kind of excellence that doesn't come from feeling good, singing a few rounds of "Kumbaya" and moving on. This level of excellence is centered on building the kind of environment in which talent insists that everyone plays to their best ability, and grows continuously because they are invested in others and appreciate the impact your organization has on them. In other words, your organization does more than simply provide an income, it is a place that people come to live, grow, and expand their lives.

"Employee engagement is the purview of white-collar
workers with cushy jobs."

Try telling this to the U.S. Marine Corps or the cashiers at Trader Joe's who have worked there an average of 18 years. Our line workers tend to be the majority that raises or lowers the expectations of our customers. The disengaged are the ones that make faulty ignition switches, which can kill people and damage the reputation of the organization. They turn their backs on customers. They don't care.

These are also the very workers that we must train to change if they are to remain vital members in our culture. They are on the front lines. They take calls from irate customers or stand on their feet all day.

They run forklifts from dawn to sunset and drive trucks through every imaginable neighborhood. Not only do they hold the biggest hand in our ability to engage customers, they can be the ones who make the products we treasure or the ones that break in our hands during the first use. In the category-leading workforce, the CEO recognizes their power and empowers them fully. And, at that moment when a product isn't working and the customer is under pressure to get it fixed, they smile, they tell us everything will be okay, and it actually *is* okay. As a customer, we walk out the door feeling satisfied and acknowledging ourselves for picking the right brand, the one with the great people who go to any lengths to provide excellence in quality and service.

"There isn't enough time or resources to create an engagement culture."

When a culture is disengaged and its talent isn't adept with change, leadership finds itself constantly putting out fires, trying to woo back customers, laying off workers, and alienating critical talent. This is often the time that valuable talent development gets axed because CEOs with axes tend to start hoarding money and cutting costs. This logic is opposite of what is needed, which is critical strategic investments that will help them stabilize and regain footing. Most do this to keep the shareholders off their backs, but occasionally the axe legitimately has to fall. The axes even fall in high-performing organizations, but those events tend to be a seismic shock because they so rarely occur.

Richard Branson offers sound advice on this topic:"Train people well enough so they can leave. Treat them well enough so they don't want to."[1]

When a CEO leads the culture and makes the engagement solution a part of the culture, bringing it "in house," the company is in the strongest position. Develop our people so well that they can work anywhere, and surprise them by being their best employment option; this combination creates the type of loyalty and enthusiasm that takes an organization to greatness.

In many cases, time should be invested in building rather than trimming. Often, it is difficult for a CEO to hear this when in the midst of a business crisis. However, that is typically when vision, communication, transparency, engagement, and a strong culture will be the only things that can pull the organization through.

"Create a strong consumer brand and the rest will follow."

In modern business, the employer brand has become as important as, and in many cases *more* critical than, the consumer brand. A case in point that most everyone will recognize is Yahoo. When a top-tier graduate comes out of Stanford, Georgia Tech, or Carnegie Mellon, they are most often looking to become an employee with Apple, Google, Facebook, and other tech leaders. Essentially, the real competition for this talent is entrepreneurism. They are not even thinking of Yahoo. In fact, many of them would consider joining Yahoo as a career killer. Consequently, Yahoo has a dim future.

Marissa Mayer's strategy for bringing Yahoo back was centered on acquisitions with which she could gut the talent to shore up the bench strength of Yahoo. Let me repeat that: she bought other companies to recruit enough talent to keep Yahoo running.[2] What was its cost of talent acquisition? Unfortunately, her team did little to change the employee culture and the employer brand. In the technology world, it is easy to understand how talent directly impacts brand. But strong employer branding, the kind that attracts the best talent in any industry, can spell the critical difference between profit and failure.

For a CEO that has built his or her previous success on consumer focus, changing their mindset can be difficult and yet, like anyone else, no CEO is immune to the pitfalls and breakthroughs associated with personal change, the very skills we are promoting here. More pointedly, everyone reading this book is human, with all of the attendant shortcomings, the ability to make up erroneous stories, to stretch the truth and shrink-wrap the results around our comfort zone. That's what humans do.

As I have shared, we learn nothing of real value by studying dysfunction. We learn our greatest lessons by studying success. I don't spend too much time studying organizational and leadership failures. They all have the similar problems that were not solved in time or on time. So what are the common threads among CEOs who lead highly engaged cultures?

Every year, Glassdoor conducts a national vote from employees on its CEOs.[3] Here are this year's top five. They have several common themes across the board with the addition of some wonderfully unique characteristics:

#1: Bob Bechek, Bain & Company—99 percent

In an industry that is not particularly known for its transparency, management consulting firm Bain & Company treats it as a critical part of its culture. As an employer brand, Bain is recognized as a company in which someone can rapidly grow. Much of the continual growth that takes place among all Bain employees is based on a strong and sophisticated mentorship program. There is little life balance. Bob Bechek came up through the ranks and has an extraordinarily strong reputation as a brilliant leader.

"I think the reality of power and influence and getting things done is overwhelmingly about informal authority nowadays," Bechek argues. "New MBAs should be focused on how to develop the skills associated with that. But the reality is, even in my current role, the vast majority of what I do is exerted through information and not formal authority. If you're involved in trying to get people galvanized around a particular course of action—or to feel inspired about what we're trying to do or feel appreciated, motivated, and valued—that has almost nothing to do with formal authority."[4]

#2: Scott Scherr, Ultimate Software—99 percent

I periodically work with Ultimate Software and find its talent personifies the very word. Its people are smart, enthusiastic, grateful, outgoing, and happy, and demonstrate the highest performance and service standards. The company has a stellar 97-percent customer retention rate. Virtually every client organization that uses Ultimate Software is somewhat religious about the experience. Much of this loyalty is based on effective and enthusiastic employees. It is the only employer in the top five to place great emphasis on work/life balance. Recently, Mr. Scherr said, "I feel humbled. I think [employees] trust me to take care of them and their families."[5]

A member of *Fortune* magazine's 100 Best Places to Work issue, Ultimate Software makes it a point to start on the right footing with an elaborate onboarding process that includes trips by every new employee to its Miami headquarters.

#3: Dominic Barton, McKinsey & Company—99 percent[6]

Not known for its work/life balance, McKinsey invests in the professional development of its people more than any other company in the management consulting industry. Combined with full transparency, McKinsey and Barton's leadership presents the ideal home for ambitious and hard-charging professionals.

A large cadre of newer professionals gets recruited into more lucrative positions in their second and third years, and yet the vast majority of them look back at McKinsey as the platform that launched their highly successful careers.

#4: Mark Zuckerberg, Facebook—98 percent

Many of the employees speak of Mark Zuckerberg and Sheryl Sandberg's humility, their willingness to listen, and their commitment to create a fully open and transparent culture. One employee said, "It might be easy to roll your eyes when people say how open their culture is, but it's true, it's more open than any other place I've worked at."[7]

Zuckerberg has said:

> Find that thing you are super passionate about. A lot of the of the founding principles of Facebook are that if people have access to more information and are more connected, it will make the world better; people will have more understanding, more empathy. That's the guiding principle for me. On hard days...that's the thing that keeps me going.[8]

Zuckerberg's leadership style includes great passion, instilling purpose in everyone at Facebook; he is utterly committed to the company's people and to the product.

#5: Jeff Weiner, LinkedIn—97 percent

The downside of LinkedIn's culture is, once again, work/life balance and strikingly few workers over the age of 40.

These technology and consulting giants work in environments with extreme change impacting every worker virtually every single day. Jeff Weiner is loved for producing a culture that pushes growth. The first question asked after a new hire or promotion is, "What is your next play?"

Weiner's most telling interview was on SuperSoul Sunday with Oprah Winfrey. He tells her the greatest advice he received from his mentor Ray Chambers, a Wall Street icon who pioneered the leveraged buyout and who later walked away from financial success to study happiness and pursue a life of philanthropy.[9] He shared Ray's five principles of happiness:

- Live in the moment.

- It's better to be loving than to be right.

- Be a spectator to your own thoughts, a fundamental key to compassion.

- Be grateful for at least one thing every day.

- Be of service to others.

• • • • •

Our top five CEOs have several traits in common. But, there is one that overrides all others: none of them take shortcuts.

Additionally, each CEO drives the following characteristics and values:

- A fully engaged culture and a superior employer brand.

- The best possible products and services, or excellence at every turn.

- The organization makes the world a better place.

- The organization makes every attempt to fully engage with every customer.

- There is simply no substitute for human decency, compassion, understanding, and a pursuit for "the high road."

Let's examine an elephant in the room. In many cases, working at a category-leading organization precludes any sense of work/life balance.

Some of our examples include organizations that put a great deal of through into helping employees establish a strong balance with raising families, pursuing personal interests and having regular "time out." In many cases, work/life balance isn't part of the equation and yet, the employees are highly engaged and praise the CEO. When we examine these cultures, we always find transparency, mentorship, strong change skills, and strong at-work relationships. Many of the people who work in environments like this view work/life balance as another fad. Engaged workers get more done in shorter periods of time. Engaged workers also tend to be engaged in every other aspect of their life. The more awakened we become, the more skilled we can apply to drawing boundaries, getting others to help us, and being strategic in how we want to live.

I asked colleagues and clients alike to recommend one person who embodies all of the characteristics of an Engagement CEO. One name kept coming up: Adam Miller from Cornerstone OnDemand. The company first came to my attention when my colleague Mary Campbell moved USC's entire learning and development division onto a digital platform. It was a daunting and complex project that shifted 25,000 employees into virtual learning and development. Cornerstone provided the platform, which became one of the biggest online learning programs in the academic world. Mary was thoroughly won over by the consistency in Cornerstone's performance, service, and sophistication. Cornerstone's 95 percent customer retention record during a 12-year history is unmatched and endemic of an awakened workforce.

My colleague Kim Shepherd is one of the more visible leaders in the digital-based talent world. She endorsed Adam as an individual who built a category leader through walking the talk, transparency, and authenticity.

Adam Miller began the company in his apartment with his two friends Perry Wallack and Steven Seymour. Today, Cornerstone OnDemand helps many of the world's largest companies recruit, train, and manage their people. More than 27 million users in 191 countries and in 42 languages engage with its software and services. Cornerstone has become one of the world's premier resources in continuous learning and development.

We arrived at a building complex that is typical of the playfulness and interactive environments so common among tech leaders. The employees caught my attention. Everyone looked us in the eye and smiled, everyone who directly engaged with us was genuinely interested and interesting. The energy was positive, comfortable, and upbeat.

Adam Miller was named Entrepreneur of the Year by Ernst & Young in 2011 and CEO of the Year by the Southern California Technology Association in 2009. He lives in Los Angeles with his wife and three children. He often tells the media that becoming a father became the wake-up call that pushed him to make Cornerstone as successful as possible, because time away from his children had better count.

We joined Adam in his office with Deaira Irons from marketing, a recent addition to the team who personifies all the company looks for: bright, alert, interested, and kind.

I gave them an overview of what is happening with employee engagement and why the global numbers are so dismal.

> **Adam:** You mean they can't keep up with the changes in their jobs?
>
> **David:** They can't! Most of the existing processes to end disengagement are like using a teaspoon to put out a fire. The ability to personally transform is the new game in being relevant for any length of time, and until we help all workers build the skills of self-change, matters will only get worse.
>
> **Adam:** We're in the 13 percent.
>
> **Mary:** You built this on a different philosophy than many companies out there.

I read the characteristics of an Engagement CEO.

> **Adam:** There is one missing characteristic.
>
> **David:** What's that?
>
> **Adam:** Shows respect towards all employees and learns from all of them.
>
> **David:** Were you like this your whole professional life?

Adam: I worked in investment banking years ago, and it was the antithesis of tech culture. It is more of a feudal system where you become a leader by how much money you make rather than how you treat people.

Mary: Punish the serf in the way you were punished when you were one.

Adam: Exactly. You would give people literally busy work. People would get assignments on Friday afternoons and told it had to be finished on Sunday afternoon or Monday morning. Many were expected to work all-nighters once a week or multiple times in a week. I remember coming into the office when it was smaller and one of the developers was bragging that he had stayed up all night. I told him that if he did it again, he would be fired and that people are never productive when they pull 20 hours. Much of what he wrote would have to be rewritten because he was so exhausted.

This culture with Cornerstone really began in the beginning and it was in opposition to what I had witnessed. We were committed to a balanced workplace. It was a little bit later in our existence where we articulated our culture. When we had 30 people, we knew we had a culture but it hadn't been defined. There was a turning point when we had 50 and would triple that number by the year end. New people would outweigh us 2 to 1. We formalized the culture. That began with the kind of people who work here who are smart, cool, dependable, and visionary. We believe in teamwork and client success. We were very clear about that, and then over time, found ways to infuse those qualities throughout the organization in how we hire people, how we develop them, how we fired people, how we did performance reviews, and how we recognized others.

David: You were directly involved in all of the early hires.

Adam: Yes. I hired the first 250 people. I personally hired all of them. After 250, it became impossible. My job became entirely interviewing.

I stopped hiring the individual contributors and hired the managers...we have over 2,000 employees, so it just isn't feasible to continue hiring employees. I do the final interview for people that are critical for representing the company in certain ways.

David: How do you hire people that are going to protect your culture DNA?

Adam: Early on, I hired the managers. I selected the ones that would hire others. I loosened up when they proved themselves. For a while, I was the last interview. By the time they got to me, they were already meeting performance and technical requirements. But, I rejected quite a few candidates, almost always on culture fit. Periodically fights brewed about that because it was so hard to find someone. But that persistence built the standards.

Mary: It is rare, uncommon that at the top of the organization, the quality of the culture is viewed as such a significant asset where they are often primarily focused on other strategic elements. So, they push those culture pieces over to the human resources and talent people. The results are an ill-defined and squishy culture.

Adam: Our talent professionals are among the best brand ambassadors for Cornerstone because they are the ones doing a wonderful job of finding and attracting the talent we need to join our team. They are the ones upholding performance management and growth. Other things we did in our early days set the standards. We had a top performer who I fired because they were a bad culture fit. That was the first time when people took culture seriously. Here was a top asset that was not a fit with us. It didn't matter. It was established early on that the team is more important than the individual.

David: In an earlier interview, you said that by opening in Los Angeles you were put in the position of having to hire potential rather than experience.

Adam: Absolutely true.

David: Is it the same way?

Adam: It is a little less true today because tech has grown in LA. But when we began, B2B marketing and software development were extremely difficult to find in LA. We found it was better to find the people with the right competencies and build their technical skills. We did this by only hiring people that were active learners. You describe this need throughout the world. Well, it is more true in a tech company. It is exponentially truer in a hyper-growth company where we have to find people who are capable of moving up from the baseline. Most tech companies don't operate that way. In hyper growth, they regularly pull out the individuals that are not keeping up with the growth. The way we did it here, the reason we have had such stable and high retention is that we hired people that required the same characteristics of active learning and in interest in personal growth. We hire the ones who demonstrate they want to learn and are ambitious. As a result, they have grown with us.

Mary: I bet you had some casualties.

Adam: Very few. It could be said that we defy the odds because in so many organizations, only one or two will make it because they are exceptional. I am saying the opposite. Only one or two did not make it because everyone had the attributes. Our people make it because they are continuous learners when they arrive as well as in the parochial process, because these are the people that get promoted.

David: What would you suggest to your client companies that have significant challenges around employee engagement and change?

Adam: I'm in agreement with you. You have to start at the top. In a world where Millennials are expected to have four to six careers in their lifetime, it has to be a place to keep learning and developing. It can't be a place where you were hired for a single job and expect to stay in that spot forever. There also has to be a major shift that happens in the corporate world, historically, where managers identify people they want on their team, you develop them and you keep them. In a world where people are expected to have multiple careers, you cannot have management push people into their box and keep them in that box. Early on, we identified that we were going to promote mobility and encourage mobility throughout the organization. At Cornerstone, that mobility is geographic where someone is not only able to move anywhere in the United States but [in] the world. It is divisional where someone can move from department to department within a division but also cross-divisional mobility where someone can move into an entirely different area of the company. We have had Millennials and Gen-Xs move throughout the entire organization in many different positions at times where in another organization they would have had to quit in order to grow.

David: You must have an incredibly transparent organization for that to work.

Adam: It took time because the managers were at first very resistant but again, we grow for the culture; we promote for culture and our people learn, especially our executives today, that mobility works for the organization as well as most of the people in it. A few leave but more come.

Mary: Academia has an enormous problem in this area. These institutions attract some of the world's best talent but they are resistant to sharing. The hoard their best so many of them...

Adam: Leave.

Mary: So many organizations could protect their best talent by providing them with options.

David: The reason so many people have difficulty with change is because they have significant deficits in what many organizations dismissively call "soft skills." Here we frame these skills as the ability to draw healthy attention to one's self and give healthy attention to others. We find it in the ability to build effective professional communities within and outside the organization.

Adam: The company can certainly enable these skills; they don't have to wait for an employee to take the initiative. We view these as crucial management skills and expect them to help their employees to develop the skills of collaboration, mentorship, peer communication, connecting with other parts of the organization, and getting others to help them. Many managers have these skills but some require training. Periodically a manager has to be removed. We expect our managers to be good role models and mentors. I have a strong belief in the player/coach model.

David: We have been studying the role of mentorship in AA and believe organizations have a lot to learn from it as a success model. Here we have an entity that has no organization, no fees, no leaders, no real structure, and yet it has continued to grow and succeed for decades.

Adam: Well you are coming from a "pay it forward" mentality. Building relationships and continuously building our teams is a central part of our culture. Recently, a senior executive got married and I noticed in the wedding pictures that over half the guests were from our company. That is the norm.

David: In the years since you launched this company to today, what have been your most difficult lessons about talent?

For a moment, he went inward and we could see him scrolling through the years. Suddenly, a cloud came into his eyes. He was clearly pained.

Adam: We had one situation between two employees that went south...we had a very painful situation on our hands.

David: I learned a great deal about you in this moment. You are so disciplined and consistent in building values into your business and surroundings that you answered my question with a clearly painful employee relations event. Most CEOs would have so many or be so out of the loop that it wouldn't cross their mind. One human capital nightmare comes along and it rocks your world because it is so out of sync with your values?

Adam: Yes.

David: What else did you learn that was difficult?

Adam: It is always a balancing act to satisfy the needs of the shareholders and the clients and the culture. Building relationships throughout the organization is such a big aspect of success. Once a year, we take everyone for a big party on the beach. Invariably I see people at their desk working and tell them, "Let's get up and go." They respond, "No, I have something that needs to get finished." I come back with, "No, this is more important." Maybe we push a deadline back one day and make it more important for people to get to know each other. That doesn't happen in a lot of companies."

Mary: It doesn't. You dragged that employee away from something that he was conditioned to treat as more important than his own opportunity to bond and connect. I bet he came back full, energized, and deeply engaged.

Adam: It requires long-term thinking. You have organizations that tell a candidate, "We need for you to start right away." But the candidate says, "Oh, I hoped to take some time off, get away, decompress." We tell them, "Take whatever time you need. We will still be here." We have the same point of view with flex time because you can shift time. Certain deadlines matter and others are not so critical.

David: What would you like us to know before we leave?

Adam: When we were a small company, we probably had about 40 people. Every year we would do something on our anniversary trip. We had no money. We asked everyone to write down a list of the perks they would want if we did have money. What order would you want them in? We set early on that even as we created shareholder value that we would be socially responsible. I believe the idea of the company itself is socially responsible. Regardless, we would build a foundation. In the last five years, our foundation has given over $125 million in impact. One of the things we did early on was to give to the shareholders, employees, and the community. We would be built on balance and we have delivered on that promise. As we became more and more successful, we added much to resources that we offer, as much as any top employer in the world."

David: Do people give their time?

Adam: We do.

When someone in our company reaches seven years, we provide them with seven week sabbatical. We have a lot of people going on sabbatical. That gives a sense of how long people are with the company.

We have a competitive culture. So our people even compete in who has the "coolest sabbatical."

As the interview finished, Deaira Irons helped us gather our belongings and walked us to the lobby. I turned to her and asked, "What do you think?" She smiled broadly, "It is all true. I have worked in some great organizations but the moment I came through that door, you could feel it. You could feel the energy, the kindness, and intelligence, all of it coursing through the halls. I am new, but this place feels like home."

8

The Right Fit

"But I think that no matter how smart, people usually see what they're already looking for, that's all."

—Veronica Roth, author of *Divergent* series

We have talked about all that we can do to build engagement after we hire talent. But, how can we do a better job of hiring already-engaged talent? Our candidates come from a market that is primarily fed two obtuse messages. They go something like the following:

- During economically good times, when there is more competition for great talent, we will treat candidates and employees better.

- During economically bad times, when talent is plentiful, we will treat candidates and employees like they are expendable.

When we examine much of the turmoil in our culture today, a great deal of it is centered around people feeling like they have been marginalized and certainly this is a reflection of some of our worst moments of organizational behavior. In the midst of this landscape, how many of us have sacrificed our standards to get or keep a job—any job? Let's couple that scenario with all of the hiring managers who have never been trained on how to interview, select, and onboard highly effective talent. It helps to also recognize that candidates have been fed such negative messages during the last few years that it doesn't take much to trigger bad feelings. Unfortunately, when we leave candidates feeling fear of survival in the hands of managers with inadequate hiring skills, all bets for the right fit vanish quickly.

Years ago, I asked a friend who was still in love with her husband after 40 years, "What is the single most important thing for me to know about having a wonderful relationship?" She looked me in the eyes, grabbed my hand, and ordered me simply, "Marry well." Who we pick as our spouse represents one of the most important factors of whether or not we are going to be happy. In a similar fashion, whether or not we are going to be happy with our work depends on two critical factors:

1. The right fit.

2. Who will be my boss?

In the end, I believe that most anyone who wants a job and anyone who is looking to hire a new employee are looking for a good "marriage." We want the partnership to be effective and also pleasurable. We want to grow from the experience. We want to look forward to working together. We want to be eventually grateful for the good decision we both made to enter the partnership.

A good boss can take what reads on paper as a mediocre job and spin that into a transformative career opportunity. On the other hand, a terrible boss can ruin the best job opportunity in the world. Time and time again, I have witnessed how one bad employee can poison engagement and team productivity. However, that "bad" employee will often turn into a star when moved to an appropriate environment. Fit matters.

Right fit is an extremely critical aspect of engagement and overall productivity. So why does it get mucked up so routinely? Well, it usually begins with a CEO or business owner who doesn't lead the culture. Why would an Engagement CEO stand idly by while hiring managers make anything less-than-right-fit hires? Why would someone allow candidates throughout the market to be treated with bad or sloppy manners? An Engagement CEO builds a culture that becomes a privilege to join and the invitation to join that culture's tribe must be earned and celebrated. When this is done really well, everyone will be grateful and likely thrives in the environment.

Employers spend approximately $3,500 every time someone is hired, a figure incidentally that represents three times the amount typically spent annually on training and development. Little, if any, of these training funds are ever allocated toward creating better hiring managers. Developing managers who are savvy with interviews, who recognize their bias, and who are better able to make sound talent acquisition decisions, represents some of the greatest potential improvements we can bring to our organizations. It also supports fully engaged cultures.

Instead, hiring managers continue to sacrifice right fit to bias. Many of them define needed technical skills but fail to define necessary soft skills or "courage" skills and capacities such as personality types, morals, values and work ethic. Many never really think about the importance of manners, presentation, demeanor, demonstrated ability to change, resiliency, enthusiasm for innovation, thoughtfulness, and persistence. Therefore, they are making choices based on incomplete information. Still other hiring managers rely on even more seat-of-the-pants style thinking, such as, "I'll know it when I see it."

When I ran staffing operations in past roles, consultants would come to me upset and with the conviction that they had the right candidate for one of our positions but, alas, another candidate was offered the job. I would typically just laugh and say, "They hired a family member." At other times I might say, "When he called to tell me they hired the least likely best candidate, maybe the last one added to hit the quota, he just said, 'There was something about her' or some such nonsense." Without thinking, they were picking a family member. How many of us came from healthy, fully functional, loving, and smart families? How many of us come from families that role modeled what it means to have a great career? Though there are quite a few, they are not the norm. We typically go with how we were raised. We do what our tribe did. I was a little kid when Lady Bird Johnson was promoting a program to clean up and beautify America. Our rather mean school-teacher was standing in front of our classroom screeching, "When you see trash by the side of road what do you think of?" A kid in the back of the room said, "Home." We tend to go with home. We go with what makes us comfortable

Employee engagement begins with how well we attract, select, and hire talent. Organizations routinely spend fortunes filling jobs, but they don't think to invest in training their hiring managers to give masterful interviews, to make more skilled decisions, and to provide highly effective onboarding. Many hire employees based on characteristics that have nothing to do with the job at hand. This lack of thinking continues, and the reason it goes on is that top leadership is divorced from upholding their standards as employers.

Timothy Wilson, professor of psychology at the University of Virginia, states, "You're faced with around 11 million pieces of information at any given moment. The brain can only process about 40 of those bits of information and so it creates shortcuts and uses past knowledge to make assumptions."[1]

Harvard University researcher Mahzarin Banaji distills the point:

> Most of us believe that we are ethical and unbiased. We imagine we're good decision makers, able to objectively size up a candidate or a venture deal and reach a fair and rational conclusion that's in our, and our organization's, best interests. But more than two decades of research confirms that, in reality, most of us fall woefully short of our inflated self-perception.[2]

When a hiring manager interviews, assesses, and eventually hires new talent without any formal skill training, we must work doubly hard to build engagement in our organizations, and we unknowingly whittle down our most optimal futures. One of the central new revolutions in talent acquisition is big data and artificial intelligence. We are reaching the stage in which technology will be able to predict the candidate that is going to be the most successful in a job. The emerging technology introduces the possibility of cutting through bias and filters so that we can more effectively find the candidate most likely to succeed. Can big data become the solution for prejudice and diversity? Well, one thing is clear: it will not happen until we produce greater awareness in our managers.

Train your managers! Give them the tools to make better decisions. For relatively modest up-front costs, you will save fortunes in mismatched talent, turnover, and other engagement challenges. Give your managers the resources to evaluate candidates before the interview. Assessment instruments can give them important insights and reveal nuances about candidates. Even the smallest employer can purchase an assessment from Amazon or other providers. Also bring other managers or colleagues into the interviewing process as appropriate. Several points of view can be quite helpful in making gains and avoiding mistakes in building the bench strength of your organization.

Skills for Tomorrow

In the modern change-driven workplace, there are several new skills we ought to be looking for in all candidates. First, find people who have a strong ability to grow relationships and a track record of active learning. Look for those able to sell their ideas and concepts to others. They will demonstrate a natural curiosity about other people's needs and expectations. They are enthusiastic networkers and connectors. They see the big picture and can make a good case for people to work together. They keep track of where the world is headed. To them, active, continuous learning represents the keys to the future. They are constantly searching for new information that is relevant to their lives and their work. They take responsibility for their actions and never blame others. Their word is golden. They don't engage in negative gossip. They know how to make friends. They build support systems naturally. Many have strong sales and presentation skills. They are receptive to feedback. They praise others generously and accept praise graciously. These are often the very workers that will teach and inspire other employees to change. Many will become great mentors who will sustain, strengthen, and grow your culture.

The last war for talent was at its peak between 2004 and 2007. As we go back to war, the game has changed so thoroughly that we need to revolutionize virtually every aspect of finding and onboarding talent. Ten years ago, our definition of right fit was very different than it is today. We fixated on such fading things as loyalty and long-term commitment. Today, we need a more sophisticated and far more candid treatment of right fit in any setting. It starts by acknowledging that things will be quite different from our past best practices.

The New Fit

The very notion of what right fit means needs to be completely transformed. Quite simply, employers that continue to operate with the notion of requiring loyalty in return for temporal jobs are not living in reality. In fact, this myth very often begins a cynical facade with employees acting as if they expect to be there for decades. Our old definitions of what right fit looks like must be traded in for a revolution in hiring practices and a new context for employment. What is the new context? Strength through diversity, and by that we are implying much more than a cross-section of race and gender. We must pursue diverse personalities and points of view. The underlying common thread doesn't need to be extraordinarily complicated. Recall that I have already mentioned that at Inspired Work, we only hire brilliant and loving people. Those two standards have more than served us well, but they also leave room for diverse skill sets, backgrounds, ethnicities, and age groups.

During the course of interviews and evaluations, we need to make every attempt to define what is motivating each candidate. Why do they want the job? What are their expectations? What drives them? The answers give us critical information and lends critical objectivity to how we populate our organizations. Ditch the loyalty and try these new employee types on for size.

The "Born to Do Its"

Every one of us has the capacity to find the work that comes to us most naturally and powerfully. It is the work that brings meaning and purpose to our lives. The "born to do it" workers have a core purpose that doesn't change. However, they consistently reinvent the way they deliver work as the world changes around them. These are the individuals that bring unique gifts to the organization, and that produce innovation and change when needed. They are not particularly loyal to their employer, but they are loyal to their particular gifts. Grow them or lose them. Identify this through their narrative as well as how they answer questions such as:

- Do you have a unique gift? If so, how would you describe it?

- What do you want to accomplish in your career?

- If we were to hire you, what would be the ideal way to package and use this gift of yours?

These individuals provide the *foundation* for their employer's brand.

The "Grew Into Its"

The rate of change today indicates that we can literally grow into another person rather quickly. A growth-oriented individual takes a job to accelerate their learning and to become more valuable. This person will regularly outgrow what they do and how they do it. The "grew into it" individuals are creative, ambitious, and adaptable.

I previously mentioned working with a large bank in the early 1990s. They were breaking down and thousands of employees were coming through our Inspired Work programs. The chief human resources officer asked for a meeting. She opened it with the question, "What is our biggest human capital problem?" I responded, "It has already taken place. The consulting firm working with the CEO has introduced one alienating concept after another. As a result, your creative and adaptive employees are gone. They pulled out their Rolodex and started calling friends. They said, 'Get me out of here. This isn't fun anymore.' The rest are hanging on for dear life."

Creative and adaptive professionals course through all of our "fit" types. These are the very people you want to treat so well that they stay and help everyone else change also. "Grew into its" use the enormous rivers of information to grow quickly. Their knowledge doubles every few years.

A few questions to get at this:

- How did you get from point A, your graduation, to point B, today?

- You seem to be eager to learn. What do you want to learn next?

- How would you bring this commitment to continuous learning to our team?

"Grew into its" are the individuals who bring *growth and innovation* to workplaces.

The "On My Ways"

When someone defines what they truly want to do in the world, it can trigger the realization that this doesn't align with the individual's current job. Some of my colleagues would call this a "lily pad" employee. Many employers are afraid that if they help someone realize their purpose, the individual will simply walk out the door. That might be true to a degree in the traditionally disengaged workplace. But, when we make it safe for our employees to discuss their true ambitions, we are also given the very information that allows us to be more supportive of them as we leverage what they bring to the table. This kind of culture also helps us identify individuals that are actively pushing disengagement.

Give these "on my ways" the room to work towards their dreams. Help them connect their progress at your organization to the progress they need to see in the big picture. If you do, your organization will become known as one that supports people and their growth, wherever that may lead. People desire and respect such employers.

A few questions for these types:

- Why do you want this job?
- How does this position fit into your long-term career plans?
- What do you really want to do with your life?
- Let's get this out on the table: if this is where you are headed, how could this opportunity give you the fuel to get there?

This worker represents the *bread and butter* of the workplace and often brings great value.

Some managers take "on my ways" and set up the circumstances for future aspirations to manifest without them having to move on out.

I know a learning and development executive who works for one of media's most iconic organizations. Every year, she hires a new assistant. On the first day she tells them, "You have one year to either promote up to a new position or leave the company." Although this is a pretty bold, even frightening, proposition, the organization is filled with producers, directors, managers, and creative professionals who began their careers in that assistant job. Consider how this expectation likely changes their engagement level on the first day. We need more of this—creating environments with such high expectations and genuine opportunities that our people excel and push themselves beyond their own perceived limits.

The "Happy With What I've Gots"

These employees tend to be loyal no matter the circumstances. They require our acknowledgement and praise. They are reliable and dedicated. Often, they are the individuals who take on projects without asking. They love routine, and they don't generally desire or pursue change. Unfortunately, these are often the workers who are shown the door during periods of downsizing. This sizeable portion of the workforce will need the guidance and mentoring to move with change, build institutional knowledge, and become more aware of the critical need to build the courage skills. But they are also solid in many ways.

A few questions for these folks:

- You spent 16 years at your last company. Why did you stay and what did you contribute while you were there?
- Please tell me what you are doing to grow your skills and your network.
- What are the most valuable skills you have learned in the past few years?

Remember we want segments of our talent to bring *stability* to the workplace. The "happy with what I've gots" provide this naturally. However, we must be keenly focused today more than ever before on hiring individuals that understand the need for change and continuous learning.

Employer Brand, Culture, and Tribe

For hundreds of thousands of years, human beings have been conditioned to look for, belong to, and live by the rules of their tribe. Tribal alignment is embedded in our DNA. As a result, it is useless to try to run any organization without developing a strong tribal ethos, which by modern definition is known as our employer brand.

Fortune magazine's 2015 "100 Best Places to Work" studied employers who had consistently remained on the list for more than 10 years and found these employment role models to have one common ingredient: they foster strong and rewarding relationships among their workers.[3] It's not so much about the perks themselves. The reason many employers provide high-quality dining is that eating together builds relationships. Going to the gym together helps employees bond with one another.

Strong relationships within an organization represent one of the fundamental muscles of engagement. Strong employer brands are developed through these strong relationships that consequently build engagement, unity, support, innovation, performance, learning, and growth. We have observed the phenomenon in our own engagement processes. When intact team members discover each other anew, they also become more engaged with their work and their customers.

What happens when we don't take the initiative to build the brand? We will mostly get people who view work as "just a job." BMW hires driving enthusiasts. Southwest Airlines hires "fun." Apple hires creative mastery. But it is useless to pursue employer branding unless the organization is willing to walk the talk. Any real employer branding initiative must be rooted in truth and authenticity. We buy products, employers, and services through faith. Without consistency, there is no faith. Without truth there is no consistency.

Here are a few elements that nourish any successful employer brand.

1. The tribe is thoroughly defined and communicates with such transparency that outsiders looking in get a full sense of what it is like to work there.

2. The brand is based in truth so that leaders and employees can support it without adopting inauthentic and temporary behavior.

3. The organization is continually improving its efforts in pre-boarding, on-boarding, developing, and retaining employees.

4. The employer brand is developed by all leaders and consequently embraced by everyone in charge.

5. The brand attracts the very people who fit into the tribe.

America's best workers look for organizations that deserve their faith. They look for organizations that pique their interest. They research the hell out of them. The rest—the individuals who are still rooted in survival and predictability—will blindly walk in the door and engage in the dance of mediocrity. So spend the time and effort to do right by your employer brand. Employees win, new candidates win, and the organization also wins.

The Great Pre-Boarding Failure

As we will discuss in the interview excerpts that appear later in this chapter, pre-boarding and on-boarding workers have become tony business processes. But the vast majority of employers are doing a terrible job of presenting their brand and creating goodwill during the hiring process. Many of my individual clients are looking for new jobs and they bring back war stories that are simply jaw-dropping. One senior executive with solid skills applied to and interviewed with 11 organizations. He made it to the final rounds with five of the companies. One got back to him with an offer. The others didn't send notes or return calls. In two cases, he had invested about 10 hours of interview time and only found out later that he didn't move forward because *he* called the recruiter. In another case, a senior executive was rounding up offers. The one she most wanted led to a verbal offer from the man who would have been her boss. She accepted the position and never heard from him again.

As you will hear from our many talent management executives, these are not unusual stories. Speak to virtually anyone who has gone through the interview experience in the last five years, and he or she will give you the name of the many companies whose treatment lacked even a modicum of respect and perhaps only one or two organizations that provided a superior experience, whether or not they got the job. These impressions are lasting and create a word-of-mouth reputation that ranges from positive to poisonous. For those candidates who do get hired, know that they will be bringing those bad experiences with them into their early days of employment. So much wasted opportunity.

Employer brands rely on an underpinning of professionalism and respect throughout the hiring process. Without kindness and consideration, we dilute, weaken, and corrupt our employer brands. A good engagement philosophy is based on the premise that employers treat their workers with the same degree of respect with which they treat their customers, and that means potential customers as well, which all candidates are before they get hired. Talent acquisition isn't much of an honorable profession if we find ourselves treating people like cattle.

Predictive Analytics

The well-known story of the Boston Red Sox has become a big shot across the bow of the talent acquisition profession. In early 2013, the team was coming off of a disastrous season, so bad that sold-out games became a thing of the past. Ownership had shed $270 million worth of payroll by trading superstars such as Adrian Gonzalez, Carl Crawford, and Josh Beckett to the Los Angeles Dodgers. General manager Ben Cherington could have easily gone after more superstar players, but instead he used predictive analytics to identify unheralded players like slugging first baseman Mike Napoli, outfielder Shane Victorino, back-up catcher David Ross, and relief pitcher Koji Uehara.[4]

The predictive analytics industry touts the Red Sox phenomenon as evidence that it can solve virtually every problem in business. While analytics has the potential to transform workforce planning, candidate selection, and employee development, the talent management leaders in our interviews suggest that we should not put our necks on the line with analytics just yet. But given a few years of development, big data could transform the practice of selection and hiring.

Predictive analytics has the *potential* to essentially remove hiring bias in a very short period of time. The process of accumulating vast quantities of data to predict which candidate is going to be most successful in a particular job offers a future where we make a big leap forward with right fit decisions.

Voices From the Front Line

We put the elements of employer brand, right fit, and the attraction/selection process in front of several talent management leaders, and they had much to share about the new world and how it plays into the game of employee engagement. Our interviews revealed the following insights from this impressive list of professionals:

- **Angela Gardner, partner, Heidrick & Struggles.** Angela currently leads assignments across the consumer markets and media, entertainment, and digital practices. Formerly, Angela built a sophisticated, from-the-ground-up talent acquisition organization for Fox and led executive recruitment for Yahoo.

- **Kim Shepherd, CEO, Decision Toolbox.** Recognized as a pioneer in the virtual workplace, Kim leads one of the world's most innovative recruitment firms. A noted public speaker and author, Kim is active in a variety of philanthropic and entrepreneurial professional associations. Her firm has received the Alfred B. Sloan Award for Excellence in the Workplace three times. In 2013, Kim was named the National Association of Women Business Owners (or NAWBO)–Orange County's Innovator of the Year.

- **Jackson Lynch, president and founder, 90consulting.** A human resources executive with an extensive background in growing organizations and leading human capital efforts during mergers and acquisitions, Jackson brings expertise from PepsiCo, Nestle, and Clearwater Paper Corporation. Over the years, Jackson Lynch has become a sought-after human resources executive who manages to link the best of human capital with profit performance. He is the founder of 90consulting, which provides human capital support to CEOs and equity investment groups.

- **David Yudis, PhD, CEO, Potential Selves.** As vice president of talent management, learning, and development at Disney Consumer Products, David developed an array of successful C-level executives. A highly polished professional, David integrates advanced education in psychology, business, and learning to build talent and leadership. He has led talent acquisition and talent development initiatives in a wide variety of environments.

David H.: How would you describe the current state of hiring and the changes that have hit this particular wheelhouse, especially compared to what was happening over the last 10 years?

Kim: In today's landscape, it is time to assume nothing in the hiring process. One size no longer fits all. Eight years ago, this was a candidate-driven market. For seven years, it was an employer-driven market. Now, the market is driven by technology.

David H.: What do you mean?

Kim: Today's savvy candidate has instant access to real-time information about an employer. They go to Glassdoor to hear from the employees. Yelp provides a voice from customers. They get the truth from CareerBuilder. Supply and Demand provides full information on your real worth in any market. Employers live in a world of total transparency.

David H.: If that is the case, why are so many hiring practices mediocre to terrible?

Kim: It is another example of the extreme disengagement that filters through much of the workplace. According to our research, over 70 percent of employers create ill will during the hiring process. It is at their own hands.

David Y.: In the last few years, I have led talent acquisition initiatives and I have also been a candidate, so I've been on both sides of the fence. As a candidate, I've been appalled by experiences with many employers. There seems to be an attitude among many organizations that if you are a candidate, you are just a commodity. They are so stretched with resources that communications are thin to say the least. I was stunned at how impersonal many of the contact points were within organizations during what is, for the candidate, a deeply personal experience. These bad experiences leave deep impressions.

Kim: Most employers need to take a course in good manners. It takes a moment to send an email to every single person that contacted the company. There is a very simple standard to follow in building a strong and seamless hiring process: "Do unto others [as you would have them do unto you]."

Angela: I'm in complete agreement with David and Kim. The lack of effective pre-boarding and on-boarding processes turn many people off before they even begin. If you treat people with disrespect, you increase the probability they will not respect their jobs. At Fox, we created a seamless hiring and non-hiring process. We began by surveying the people we hired and didn't hire to examine the perceptions we were creating in the market. The employer brand we create during the talent acquisition experience isn't a functional issue. It is a matter of culture.

David H.: Angela, whenever you use the word "culture," it seems you are signifying something that needs to come from the CEO or owner.

Angela: Absolutely. A lackadaisical attitude towards the employer brand from the CEO sentences the organization's employer brand to mediocrity. When the person in charge makes employer brand and culture [the] number one [priority], everyone else works on the directive with intention. Develop the culture and the tribe until you can clearly articulate it to everyone and anyone. Not thinking it through is one of the most common business mistakes and the results will be brutal. Everyone knows! Everyone sees it.

David Y.: I don't believe that many companies intend to create bad experiences in the interview process. The problem stems from CEOs who believe the employer brand and the culture is someone else's job.

Jackson: Every company is going to have a culture, so the notion that you should passively let it happen to you doesn't make sense to me. If a CEO is trying to only drive short-term profits, they are unlikely to invest in building culture, and as such, the strength of engagement will be weaker almost every time. The company, however, will still have a culture. It just won't be the one that attracts people who are committed to and passionate about enterprise success. We have lived with this model of short-term profits for a long time and the results continue to be mediocre. I am in agreement with everyone at the table and yet setting strategies and policies that offer seamless and effective talent acquisition will require soul-searching for a variety of CEOs. Walking the talk will require many organizations to change their rewards systems. Many compensation packages are in direct conflict with building value. When we send a message through an organization that no matter how well you do, no matter how much value you bring to the table, you can be gone in a moment, why would anyone engage?

Kim: A simple and common-sense approach for employers is to answer the questions, "Who do you want to be? Is it intentional?" When I became the CEO of Decision Toolbox, I was looking for singular works and standards to drive the culture. I selected the word "respect." All types of culture qualities came out of the word. For example, we live by the ethos of "on time." Everyone is expected to be on time with clients, candidates, team members, and meetings. A second late is not acceptable. When we have a meeting, 200 team members around the world are expected to be on time. If we start a webinar at 11, I can log on at 10:59 and see every single member of the team is ready to go...."

David H.: In the last 10 years, what skills have become much more important across the board?

Jackson: I'm always looking for active learning skills. Jobs become so obsolete so quickly that we need employees who recognize the need for continual learning, who have curiosity and take personal responsibility for staying competitive.

David H.: How do you find that?

Jackson: Ask the right questions:

- Give me a learning experience. Now, apply that experience to a current problem.

- What was the last book you read?

- How did that book make you a better CEO?

Angela: I agree, but we also need managers who recognize the need for learning, who lead personal change. Work environments and expectations can change in a millisecond. Today, expectations are much more fragile. If the managers are not especially communicative, if they are not role models in personal learning, half the team can have a foot out the door."

David H.: Kim, I wince every time I hear the words "soft skills." It requires more courage to become a good communicator and relationship builder than learning a new software package. The words "soft skills" have often been used in a rather dismissible manner.

Kim: I've noticed that, but it doesn't let them off the hook. One of the most important questions virtually every employer ought to ask is "How effective is this person at developing relationships?"

Jackson: Engagement begins with the relationship you have with your manager. Anyone in a leadership capacity needs the skills of developing strongly effective bonds with their workers. We've all heard the airline pilot say, "I know you have a choice of airlines, so thanks for flying ours." When was the last time you heard your manager say the same thing about working for your company?

David H.: As well as the ability to change oneself?

Jackson: Of course, but that ability is just starting to reveal its importance.

David H.: We've discussed employer brand and the initial talent acquisition process. We have been finding that one of the single biggest breakdowns is with the hiring managers. Many have never been taught how to conduct an interview. Many hire with bias and are not even aware of their bias. What are your thoughts?

Kim: Fortunes in recruitment time and costs are lost every day because managers are often lousy interviewers. In most cases, the problem can be resolved with a little bit of training and coaching. However, the vast majority of employers don't offer this to their managers and, in smaller organizations, few take the initiative to get trained. Unfortunately, smaller employers need this the most because they don't have much wiggle room with hiring mistakes.

David H.: What about bias?

Kim: It goes on every single day and undermines good hires. I would suggest that we replace the word "bias" with "ignorance."

David Y.: As I have developed high-potential executives for C-level positions, getting them to understand bias and how it influences their selection and development of talent represents a fundamental shift in their ability to lead.

Jackson: It isn't enough to have a strong recruitment team while still having a mediocre onboarding process. Consider talent acquisition as a seamless supply chain. Then, find the truth about the strengths and weaknesses in each link. If we find that our managers have big shortcomings with their hiring decisions, train them to do better or enable them to rely on data rather than gut feel.

Angela: It is helpful to train hiring managers to do more than just conduct a good interview. When we had larger recruitment projects, we would actually create war rooms and bring hiring managers to work on the recruitment process. We showed them how to find candidates on LinkedIn and create a more vital kind of outreach. As we develop managers to make good hires, it is wise to give them understanding in generational differences and finding out what people really want.

David H.: Predictive analytics have the potential to eliminate much hiring bias and help managers make much better hiring decisions. Are we there yet or does this resource require more development?

Kim: Of course it requires more development, but we love it. We use analytics to drive candidate flow, to help identify top candidates as well as formulating compensation for each team member.

David H.: Compensation?

Kim: Our analytics measure a wide range of performance factors with each team member. A few, for example, include time to filling position, accuracy with candidate selection, customer satisfaction, and repeat business. These are the drivers behind Decision Toolbox's growth.

Angela: For hiring decisions, not one company is close to using it effectively out in the real world.

David H.: Are you saying technology has yet to develop intuition?

David Y.: Predictive data is not an answer in itself, but it offers a means to refine our decisions. Consequently, it saves cost, time, and effort. Ultimately analytics could help us with bias because hiring managers continue to represent the biggest breakdown in talent acquisition.

Jackson: Every year brings so much more capacity to analytics that we need to pay close attention to innovations. I use it widely, but doing so requires that I'm educated in today's limitations. However, the impact of big data will only grow.

Jackson: I also agree with definitions of right fit. But the vast changes that have happened in employment only elevate the need for us to coach our managers in how to identify right fit for their team. We need to locate the skills needed to do the job. We need to evaluate their raw talent for the future. We need to make sure the candidate's motivations align with the organization. We need active learners. The change is great enough that many managers have a new bias from simply being rooted in the past.

David Y.: I am in complete agreement with Jackson. I am always looking for culturally adept candidates. There needs to be a work and role fit but it can't stop there. We need to ask the question, "Can you be one of us?"

David H.: During a leadership program at Disney, one of the executives asked me what I felt the Disney employer brand was. I blurted out, "Disney is all about creating magic at great profit in the midst of chaos." A collective gasp rose from the room and then laughter. If you happen to love generating a lot of money-making magic with chaos around you, you will want to be there forever.

David Y.: That is a great example. Each tribe has its own look, feel, dress, rituals, hours, and mission. Will this person fit in? Disney has a highly developed and unique culture. It is so strong that individuals who leave often have a difficult time letting go of it.

Jackson: Back to our managers. Don't just hire what you like. Hire people who push you out of your comfort zone. Hire people who are smarter than you. Hire people who have the ability to become great.

Kim: I am also in agreement with David's four types of right fit. The discomfort that I have is there is no "one size fits all" approach to employer brand and right fit.

Angela: Much of this conversation is about skill-building. The new workplace doesn't thrive on black and white anymore. For example, analytics can help us, but we can't afford to absolve ourselves of finding out the very real truth of each person we evaluate for our team. It requires that we assume nothing about the employer brand in our organization. This entire discussion is about becoming more skilled in surrounding ourselves with the people that fit our mission. That is the big payoff from this work.

Their contributions left me with the thought that when we really get the game right, when the attraction, selection, and development process falls together, we get to work with people like Angela Gardner, David Yudis, Jackson Lynch, and Kim Shepherd. This is the big payoff, colleagues who make us bigger, who demand the best from us and give us their all.

9

Mid-Management:
Engagement's Final Frontier

In a Harvard Business School study, mid-level managers emerged as the most disengaged of all workers.[1] This is not a big surprise. Mid-managers are overworked, undervalued, and the most at-risk employees during lay-offs. Academics and business authors routinely suggest that we get rid of them as a first step to becoming more lean and improving organizational performance. It's practically mindless at this point. It also protects the executive ranks from the impact of necessary downsizing.

Organizations have a history of adding more and more work to mid-managers. We frequently select many mid-managers because they get the job done quickly and accurately. We then promote them to manage others or to use that core strength to finish an important project. However, many do not receive management skills training, so instead of elevating to a level of management performance, they generally continue doing the work the way that led to their success. Thus, their workload goes up until they break or leave. Ongoing restructuring, the elimination of career ladders, and persistent insecurity have diluted mid-managers' loyalty. Many become demoralized and disenfranchised. Why don't we manage this group better?

In 2012, *Harvard Business Review* indicated that almost half of the Gen-Xs, which represents the largest segment of mid-managers, planned to leave their jobs within two years. A year before, Bersin &

Associates released the findings of their research and indicated that: "Middle managers have fewer resources, manage more people, and are less engaged than all other employee groups."[2] This is backwards. If we think so little of them, why do we let mid-managers lead and motivate the organization's largest number of workers, often the ones that directly touch our customers?

Take a moment to consider all of the managers in customer service call centers, grocery stores, department stores, service centers, specialty retailers, schools, insurance agencies, healthcare, and government. Now imagine that stressed, overworked, and disengaged professionals are managing the very individuals that engage with our prospective or dedicated customers. Yet we wonder why we complain about the poor customer service we experience and why it so pervasive. The problem has grown to the point that many companies routinely do nothing because the competition is exactly the same. Why change if the public hates everyone in the category? It has been normalized as something that cannot be avoided.

There is this deeply embedded organizational message that is quite clear and also destructive. We tell mid-managers to keep moving faster. We then invest far more time and money on our executives and sales teams. It's a relatively codependent way of existing. No one questions it and everyone plays along. But isn't it a little odd that the people who most influence our market interface can be treated as such an afterthought?

A Day in the Life of a Mid-Level Manager

Years ago, I was listening to a human resources manager talk about the dreadful past she had lived through. Earlier that year, the firm's headquarters tower caught fire. She was given the responsibility to handle the injured and dead team members. Her next job was to relocate more than 3,000 employees to new quarters. About three months later, a few missteps by the CEO led to laying off more than 2,000 workers, followed quickly by another 1,500. During their annual holiday celebration, they did one of those gift lotteries. She got a cheese wheel with a hatchet. Someone at the table laughed, "Isn't that appropriate."

I remember asking her if anyone, just once, had asked her how *she* was doing and she responded with a flood of tears. They were tears filled with sorrow, loss, and sheer emotional exhaustion. She had laid-off friends, colleagues, people she had known and worked with for years, and yet no one asked. The implicit message was, "You should be happy to have a job."

Mid-managers who run profit centers have many of the same issues, but they are treated far more respectfully than managers in areas categorized as overhead. This particular category often falls victim to a syndrome I call "losing one's life through competency." They become mid-managers because they solve problems quickly and effectively. They know their job and they do it well. When we promote them, they solve larger volumes of problems. Their support system, if they even have one, can rarely keep up. They work harder and faster until the day comes where they simply run out of fuel. Sound familiar?

Back then my friend from the bank was living in the era of the *One-Minute Manager*, a popular book by Spencer Johnson. The book struck a chord because it was a concept so appropriate for the times when people *were* veritable machines constantly racing towards the next quota. The pressure to keep running overshadowed the concept of right-sizing our attention based on the needs of the person in front of us.

The Morphing of the Mid-Level Manager's Role

Mid-managers were once the "jack-of-all-trades" and the watch-dogs. We went to them to solve problems and for key information. They came after us when we fell behind to fill the gaps. Today, the internet is one of the biggest competitors with middle management. There is essentially an answer for anything and it's instantaneously available. In many organizations, mid-managers are there to simply keep track of what people are doing. Today, technology does a much better job of tracking performance.

As the need for mid-management changes, there is a real opportunity for these individuals to look at life beyond the trappings of recent years and become experts, counselors, coaches, and leaders who inspire the best from everyone they touch. This is a very different role than someone who checks the boxes of productivity, which for most, especially the Millennials, is just meddlesome and irritating.

Engaged workers want and expect to be trusted. The traditional mid-manager interferes with that need. Today, the mid-manager exemplifies the type of individual that most needs to change and yet has reached a certain level of success by doing the same thing over and over, more and more quickly. Ongoing restructuring, the elimination of career ladders, and persistent insecurity have diluted the mid-managers' loyalty, as many have become demoralized and disenfranchised.

Where We Go From Here

As stated earlier, almost half of the Gen-Xs, which represents the largest segment of mid-managers, planned to leave their jobs within two years. But are they going to get better jobs? The probability is high that their next jobs might be only incrementally better or the same. And without a thought revolution, they will get more of the same.

For example, in the human resources profession, the prevailing word of caution is that you either find your way "to the table"—in other words, on par with other C-level executives—or face irrelevance. Tactical human resources positions are getting outsourced to technology. Time and time again, human resources professionals want to find their way into the senior leadership circles but will continue to fail to get their messages through to the other executives if they cannot decidedly move beyond the task-heavy and strategically weak skill sets they are more know for. They are trying, and a growing number are succeeding, but many more still need to realize breakthroughs.

Not only do mid-managers need extra support in embracing the skill-building and strategic development outlined in *The Workplace Engagement Solution*, they ought to be given additional time to change before assuming any mentorship roles. Why? Let's return for a moment to the "killer filter": frenzy.

It is unusual for mid-managers to show up to training and development programs with big smiles on their faces. They don't have time, even if the promise is that it will change their lives. Many of them work through lunch rather than proactively connecting with mentors. They simply do not have the time. The mid-management mindset that creeps into their system is about making piles of tasks and plowing through them endlessly. They can never catch up.

In other cases, mid-managers are being asked to shift supervisory activities to get back on the ground and to manage a project and make miracles happen inside a complex set of resources. Their necks are always on the line, even if they don't have direct responsibility for the project. So, in essence, the people that we are moving out of people supervision and back into project management are trudging through with a strong sense of dissatisfaction working against them. Many would likely make great executives, but we can't even evaluate a good number of them properly because they are not given access to the change and attention-focusing skills we have described in this book.

This is why leadership development ought to include everyone— democratic, complete. The current state of overload is not *their* fault; it is a collective failure of leadership coupled with a growing cynicism within the entire mid-management category. If we are not giving them the development they need to succeed in their existing roles, how will they grow and evolve into future leaders? That said, managers that see change as an opportunity will practice collaborative accountability with leadership or they will remain exactly where they are today. Otherwise, they may slip further downward under the weight of the growing pressure.

Evolving Leadership

We should point out that transforming our mid-managers into strategic, thinking, connective professionals will require full accountability on both sides of the fence. Mid-managers will have to demonstrate an almost-hair-raising commitment to change in order to let go of the "crazed worker" persona who measures all value by constant activity. In order to do that, they will have to reclaim their time.

Among the many managers I have worked with, I have often observed that they take on everything with a survival-mode vengeance, but often lack priorities in how to use their time and to get others to help them where appropriate. Many managers are in such a trance that time is used the same way high fructose corn syrup is used in the American diet as nourishment. We just keep stuffing more in.

We need to begin by helping mid-managers reclaim their time. It is so necessary to prioritize what we do with our time in ways that create the greatest value. It's important to begin each day by asking questions that help us define who most needs our attention and what we can do to move forward strategically, analyzing what kind of support would be most helpful to develop, and taking the time to truly identify how we want to use our time. For the mid-manager who seeks upward mobility, we need to make it clear that the only way this will happen is if they engage in the kind of learning that helps them move from activity to influence, and from flailing to the masterful ownership of their time.

This kind of professional tribe derives extraordinary value through consistent self-inquiry and mentoring. I find that it takes years to produce change when we simply tell someone that they must change. Transformation is far more rapid when we ask people the questions that connect them with the life they want to lead. Give them the questions that will help them connect with the habitual behaviors and beliefs that are keeping them stuck in the middle.

A few examples:

- Who most needs my attention and inspiration?
- What is the most critical problem to solve today?
- What is today's ideal blend of tactical and strategic work?
- What am I being asked to do that offers little value to the organization?
- How can I get rid of these useless, meaningless tasks?
- Which stakeholder needs my attention?
- Who deserves my praise today?
- What can I do to sell my ideas and solutions?
- How can I best take care of myself?
- How can I grow my support system?

This takes five minutes a day and it establishes priorities before the onslaught begins.

One of the real wedges against creating emotionally engaging mid-managers is the common practice of asking them to do work that doesn't advance the cause of the organization. A senior executive asks for reports and projects that are only about checking old boxes or covering one's behind. They are called into meetings that drone on and on without any real progress to show for it. Learning how to masterfully turn this work away can be nothing short of transformational. A few examples of taking a stand for use of time help us envision a better future:

> *"I would be happy to do this report, but I need you to know that if I do this the deadline for finishing your client fulfillment project can't be met. Can we discuss some alternative scenarios?"*

> *"I would love to help you, but I'm on a critical project for the president. Who else can we find to help you?"*

Some will say that they could never respond to their boss like that. Well, then this is a good time to start learning how to do that. Initially, you might have trouble with the energetic and emotional feel behind the words. Smile warmly and take a deep breath. You want the persona of someone who is there to contribute, rather than someone who is upset or uncertain.

CEOs could improve many cultures by making it clear that needless reports, superficial projects, and other wastes of time are to be set aside. Let everyone know that supervisors and managers are free to discuss the value of a project, to work with their superior in defining if it is really necessary, and if they are loaded up with work, to identify another colleagues to take on the project.

In our leadership programs, it has become clear that many people are afraid to say anything that appears to be a message of "no" in environments in which mid-managers are at risk. Once again, making individual and organization behavioral changes can only come out of collective responsibility. But the payoff, if we can do this, will be managers who are awake, energized, enthused, and fully present. If you are simply surviving by pushing them to work faster, technology is either available now or on its way that can help do that for you. The machine-like worker is rapidly becoming a thing of the past and organizations that don't see this are squandering one of the great opportunities in *The Workplace Engagement Solution.*

Train Your Managers

We need to give extra support to managers during our culture revolution. Our managers hold the biggest key to the quality of relationships with customers and frontline employees. Managers execute policy, solve emerging problems, and influence brand ambassadorship in substantial ways. If an organization doesn't get this, there may be big trouble ahead. Bad stuff can happen.

Whenever we move, the most painful portion of that move tends to be the cable company. Two years ago, we were changing locations with the same cable company, but it took four days, almost five hours of phone calls, and two visits to the local branch office to make the transition. At each step of the service change, someone wasn't paying attention, which led to interrupted service and surreal losses of time, all at the hands of a staff that seemed to be counting the minutes until they could go home. This level of disengagement is so enormous that we had factored in the insanity to our overall move.

It seems that when CEOs come to the conclusion they have a captive market and their business is a commodity, employees and managers alike are also treated like commodities, where work is "just a job" with no value to their ability to connect because they are more like machines. When this notion moves into knowledge-based companies, the need for engaged managers reaches epic proportions.

To that end, Wharton management professor Ethan Mollick has a message: "Pay closer attention to your middle managers. They have a greater impact on company performance than almost any other part of the organization."[3]

His studies point out that mid-managers contribute far more to the bottom line than the innovators, who knowledge- and technology-driven companies tend to revere. The best of the mid-managers are not just good in one organization; they are good in a wide variety of settings. This is because the best mid-managers have the interpersonal skills and discipline that impact all stakeholders in positive ways. The ones who do not have the skills of high engagement and the ability to change tend to remain glued in one place, hoping the human resources "death angel" has others to visit. But the managers with highly portable skills will leave if we don't give them the value and attention they deserve.

Our best and brightest workers are gone before many of us have come up with effective strategies for retaining them during upheaval. Mid-managers are often already so overwhelmed, they become less effective with retention during these difficult times.

Stop taking your mid-managers for granted. Teach them how to take better care of themselves. Give them the change and engagement skills, and never treat their development as remedial. Provide it to them because they deserve it. If they are starved for attention, correct the problem by giving them your attention. Look them in the eye. Many of them are your hardest workers. Many of them were happy with the recognition of that first promotion. Many are disenchanted because we stopped paying attention. We stopped giving them what they most needed: nourishment, respect, and kindness. They watch technology threaten their jobs, but we forgot how valuable they were the moment we assumed they could or would not change. We thought of them as the workhorses down the hall and forgot the truth. They need what we need. This is the truth and, as Joe Klass famously once said, "The truth will set you free, but first, it will probably piss you off."[4]

Love your managers back to wakefulness and many will become your most effective change agents. If we want the best from our workplace, this is our collective responsibility. Some mid-managers will respond to development with enthusiasm and gratitude. Some will have enthusiasm and gratitude after they experience the work. Some will have to leave because the mind blocks are so deep, they cannot hear you. One of my great joys is to visit with an intact team that has just gone through our program. The moment I walk in the door, the energy is different, the enthusiasm is palpable, and the relationships transformed. As we invest the needed energy and development in our mid-managers, this type of experience will become the norm.

In moving forward with *The Workplace Engagement Solution*, make mid-managers your priority. Remember that they touch *everything*.

And, even if they leave, remember that tomorrow's employer will not be evaluated on how much they paid employees, but rather they will be judged by how much they grew them while they were there.

10

Getting Started

The Workplace Engagement Solution represents breakthrough improvements for most cultures. Although pulling this together might seem overwhelming at first, I suggest taking more of a Japanese kaizen approach by establishing a highly defined end result and then taking incremental steps to get there. Also, be mindful to develop a "right-sized" approach that fits the size and scope of your organization. In a large, multi-national organization, for example, it will make great sense to have a team reporting directly to the CEO to implement and grow the initiative with the full weight of top leadership. Small organizations may too quickly dismiss the ideas outlined in this book. The truth is that small organizations don't have the option of making big mistakes around culture and talent; they need to be vigilant as well. The need to build engagement and an almost elite athleticism around swift, effective change is more—not less—significant.

The most appropriate approach for optimal success is for the owner or CEO to directly work with their people until a fully self-sustaining process takes shape. Though it takes an investment of time, it is time well worth the ROI it will foster in stabilizing and elevating the culture for all involved.

If you are reading this and you are not the CEO or business owner, remember this process is designed for everyone's benefit. By now, you probably understand that continual learning, courage skills, connectivity, and engagement are vital aspects of your career success and the success of any organization you may join. I suggest that you use every tool in the book; apply each skill to your own life, and important transformation will permeate all aspects of your personal and professional life.

The following are the steps to launching your own Workforce Engagement Solution.

CEO/Business Owner

Like CEO of Cornerstone OnDemand, Adam Miller, take charge of your culture. Be personally responsible and personally involved. It can be helpful to ask yourself the following questions:

- What kind of employer brand will fulfill our vision?
- What are the values, central competencies, and style of our ideal employees?
- When people hear our organization's name, how do we want them to envision our people?
- How effective is our workforce with continuous learning? What do they bring to the organization as a result?
- What is the current "engagement state" of our managers and how will we improve that?
- What are the various forms of my own personal bias?
- How will I orchestrate the change and engagement solution in my organization?

This should not be left to accidental success or haphazard failure. We need to design your workplace to fit your values and vision, but if you want productive energy and excitement, you need to push the envelope further. Stand your ground and don't compromise. Compromising will always result in partial sacrifice of your vision and, essentially, will compromise you.

Exercise: Pull out a clean sheet of paper or open a fresh screen on your device. Give it a title.

Our Future State

Based on everything you have read, what are you inspired to build? Describe the new state as clearly and as vividly as possible. When you finish the initial document, keep it in a safe place. This one will never be finished. It is only a beginning, one that you will want to update on a continual basis.

After the initial overview, answer these additional questions to help clarify every significant aspect of your engagement culture. (These questions are valuable for all members within the culture.)

1. What are the capabilities that would allow every segment of the workforce to execute their own personal change?

2. In order to build a fully engaged workplace, what kinds of changes are you going to need to make in yours and others' behavior?

3. What happens to your organization when it is filled with continuous learners?

4. What changes and improvements will bring full transparency to your culture?

Now, it is time to assemble the people that will help you. Discuss with them all that you want to accomplish and move forward.

The Book Club

Begin the journey by giving every employee a copy of *The Workplace Engagement Solution*. Establish several expectations for absorbing and applying the ideas from the book. Here are some examples of how to message the effort to your employees:

- The organization is beginning a culture development process focused on developing the skills of self-change within every employee and establishing a fully engaged culture. This is not just a culture change initiative. It is a commitment to build and expect the best of everyone within the organization. This initiative is about building a culture together that people want to join in order to grow and thrive.

- Ask for feedback from everyone based on the following seven questions:

    1. How did you react to the ideas in this book?

    2. What do you most want to learn?

    3. How do you envision growing the skills within the organization?

    4. How could this process impact you personally?

    5. Are you interested in helping to organize an effort on this within our organization?

    6. Would you be interested in becoming a mentor? If so, why?

    7. What do you hope the outcomes of this process will be?

- Have intact teams meet once per week to discuss one chapter of the book. Explore how the views impact each member of the team. If there are questions in the chapter, answer them as well as the questions from the book report introduction.

The Book Club will accomplish a great deal in preparing the organization and setting new cultural expectations. It begins a vital conversation that introduces new concepts, helps team members absorb the ideas, and allows them to begin envisioning the change process within themselves as well as in the organization. It also gives stakeholders real opportunities to voice their points of view about the process. People need time to digest and internalize the concepts and insights. It is a time period that helps natural leaders step forward to voice their enthusiasm and desire to adopt the skills and processes as soon as possible. It also gives the organization indicators about potential mentors. This is about change *with* others, rather than imposing change onto others.

Implementation Team

Continuing with the theme of "right-sizing" to your organization, the team can be as small as one or two in smaller environments. In larger organizations, the team can include the CEO, chief human resources officer, learning executive, and any other leaders that either have a strong attraction to the engagement solution or who demonstrate most of the skills. The team will be responsible for not only implementation but also with continuity and sustainability. In other words, every aspect of the solution must be built into an ongoing practice to develop the new culture and instill the genuine lasting improvement that is required.

Communications and Policy

All policy communications ought to be delivered by the CEO or business owner. Without this critical element of success, the entire process gets funky and develops a lackluster feel based on the reality of a low commitment level. Depending upon the size of the organization, there will be a variety of individuals who can help with building the process. The communications need to describe the vision and voice the new expectations. The trance, for everyone, is officially over. You are now working together to build an organization that celebrates growth, that continuously learns, and that gives high quality attention to customers, but also to colleagues, vendors, and employees themselves. Convey that everyone owns and is accountable to the new reality and will be required to demonstrate what that means in a personal way.

Self-Inquiry

Continuous self-inquiry, for most people, is extremely rare. Many people have been conditioned to seek outside stimuli and reference points rather than connecting with their *own* truth. Why? Part of the reason is that the journey inward can bring a certain discomfort. Consequently, we need good role models who can demonstrate how it is done and help to ritualize self-inquiry until it becomes a natural, comfortable part of the culture as well as an expectation for personal development within the organization. Everyone participates.

The self-inquiry processes can be built into notepad rituals and protocols as well as online formats. Exercises should include the following elements.

- Strategic and career development targets (three, six, and/ or 12 months)

- Change awareness—developing clarity around beneficial personal and collective change.

- Time value (daily)—using self-inquiry to get the most out of the day ahead.

- Positive action (weekly)—identifying the most valuable actions to take regardless of whether they come easy or with discomfort.

As the workforce engagement solution grows with practice, employees will eventually learn to administer self-inquiry, become mentors to others, and provide oversight to the process.

Learning

Drawing Healthy Attention to Oneself

Teach everyone question-driven consultative sales skills to boost their ability to connect with others' needs and expectations. Provide presentation skills training broadly so that people can learn how to present in front of others and connect with an audience. Today, presentation skills development ought to include one-on-one, speaker-to-audience, and virtual (on camera) presentations to remote audiences. Each has different needs and success drivers. The training is not to turn everyone into a sales executive, but to instill comfort and skill with varying forms of communication, attention, influence, and persuasion. One of the most important benefits of these presentations is to help each person take greater ownership of their work and apply critical thinking to what it is that they do. The process helps them apply enthusiasm to the role and if they cannot find it, reveal the need to change themselves or change their role.

To significantly boost the benefits of this work, it is relatively easy to establish a Toastmasters chapter in your organization, and it is also easy to find one in your neighborhood. By encouraging your employees to attend, their skills improve quickly through practice, feedback, and repetition.

You may opt to build learning programs that are delivered in person or online. Regardless, remember that building skills in this area only comes through practice. Make it a point to give everyone opportunities to step forward and make presentations in a variety of group settings, from one-on-one to small and large groups, and also in video environments. Encourage teams to share opportunities to make presentations at meetings and rotate members so that everyone has regular opportunities to be in front of the group. This is a tremendously powerful professional development opportunity and personal growth experience.

Support Systems and Community Building

Building support is a continuous and ongoing process. One of the best places to begin is in social networking training because this is how people network today. However, you will want a specific type of training. Teach your employees how to identify great leads for their work, their careers, and their learning, and to find new mentors. Show them how to find leads that could become valued assets for the organization. Help them learn how to communicate with far more "high-touch" methods than simply sending a generic note or resorting to high-volume impersonal mailings. Set the expectation that everyone is responsible to find new resources for themselves and the organization. Help them to think for themselves and gain a deeper understanding of the organization's success equation. For example, whenever we introduce changes to the mission, vision, and purpose, we must also generate and customize new support systems. It's about making more people capable and responsible for the critical thinking and analysis that goes beyond normal operations.

As mentors are developed within the organization, they will become a resource for developing stronger support systems with the customers and clients of the organization. Mentors will help participants develop support around personal finance, health and wellness, skill-building, mentorship, education, administration, play and leisure, childcare, risk-taking, and fear management.

The bottom line is that you need to make social networking and community building a strong part of the overall culture. With my organization's work in this area, we find that understanding the value of a strong community of support can be extremely powerful and transformative. Use it to elevate and enhance the process to improve talent acquisition, sales, and business intelligence. Create new and unique strategic partnerships and be on constant watch to identify new opportunities.

The Mentor-Driven Culture

Returning to the model of the AA mentorship culture, mentors are not derived from a caste system. For example, simply being a senior executive within an organization does not necessarily qualify someone as a role model for self-change and engagement. The title of mentor is one that must be earned. Unless the organization has a highly restrictive structure, we advise that you not make mentorship just another aspect of management. This route can corrupt the mentoring process and erase the benefits of pure mentorship throughout the organization. It can also corrupt the standards around "engagement for all."

Keep mentorship in a special category: an aspirational role that is above and beyond any job description. How many managers in their current state would make good mentors? Of course we want managers and executives with superb mentorship capabilities, but that is not a given. If we award the title without deeper scrutiny, we can compromise the qualities and the recognition that comes from earning the role. Mentoring is an art and a sacred trust. All stand to gain from the deeper exploration of what it means to do it well.

Early Adopters

Depending upon the size of the organization, seek to find individuals who naturally demonstrate many of these skills and naturally understand the concepts within this book as the people to put on a fast track. Regardless, take the most responsible and enthusiastic volunteers. Track their progress and support them in the mentoring relationship directly.

Talent Acquisition and Right Fit

No matter what size your organization, always develop an in-depth employer brand that defines the tribe and a clear understanding of the people who fit into that tribe. No matter what, create a seamless and effective talent acquisition process that identifies ideal fit at every level of the supply chain.

Strive to create an acquisition process that provides quality experiences for candidates and new hires alike. Develop talent acquisition skills throughout the organization. In many cases, hiring managers need training in how to hire to this level of performance. Provide resources that help everyone involved with talent acquisition to identify their own biases. Establish clear objectives regarding what right fit looks like. This becomes the standard. Watch for resistance in the form of old, misguided filters such as "We don't have time." Quite candidly, they often don't have the time because of the dysfunction that occurs from sloppy hiring and talent acquisition practices.

Transparency

It is important to establish full transparency around the process through workplace configuration, policy, technology, and intention. When everyone sees how others are performing it creates a natural competition, establishes baselines for performance, and builds trust. Time and time again, even simple technology upgrades offer immediate improvements with engagement and customer performance. With the advent of the virtual workplace, all types of software have emerged that measures virtually every metric of performance. At a glance, anyone can see how peers, direct reports, and superiors are performing. The spirit behind building transparency is to remove isolation in the physical workplace so that team members are seen and available to each other. Finally, "walk the talk." When senior management tells people to do something and then does not practice it personally, employees feel patronized and end up "going through the motions."

The invitation is to create a culture in which there is nothing to hide. If you can't readily see it, begin by envisioning it, wanting it, or just having the courage to go through with it. If it's still elusive, then it might be time to examine why. Security and transparency are vastly different issues and both can live peacefully together. Transparency suggests that all of us are practicing behavior and creating value that all eyes can see and connect with.

Feedback

It's simple. Establish feedback in a variety of areas.

Employee Surveys

Don't use surveys to measure complaints and criticism. If that is the current state, surveys only remind employees of why they are having so much difficulty with the culture. Use surveys to measure progress! Use them to demonstrate how the learning programs are progressing and to offer opportunities for suggestions on how to better develop your change and engagement initiatives. Use surveys to measure the quality of mentorship and performance, relationships and personal growth, and the ability to change and move forward.

Financial Feedback

Work with your finance professionals to establish straightforward methods that attach profit to engagement, customer involvement, and learning. Even better, demonstrate engagement as a profit source rather than an expense. Here is my promise: in almost all cases, you will witness that profits and customer retention closely mirror increases or decreases in employee engagement.

Measuring financial performance can also lead to much-needed revisions in your compensation structures. Measuring engagement, mentorship capabilities, and improved life skills also supports the building of a thoroughly modern and effective workplace.

Celebrate and Praise

These important drivers of success—acknowledgement, praise, and celebration—are still too often overlooked or underemphasized. You need to establish benchmarks in the growth of your workforce engagement solution. Identify the characteristics you want your employees to develop. When you see it happening, celebrate! Acknowledge everyone. Praise people that went above and beyond the expectations. Never fall into a mindless, predictable routine in this area because if someone expects when you are going to say thank you or how we are going to do it, you've already lost the special moment as well as the impact. Celebrate creatively and spontaneously. Have a wonderful time. Do it in a way that feeds your soul as much as it feeds the soul of others.

What's Possible

Let's return to the facts. Category leaders tend to attract engaged workers. But, if only 13 percent of the world's workers are engaged, any other organization that hopes to excel must build engaged employees. It will not be enough to simply pay them more because without the culture development, the organization will continue to disengage their talent. For those who roll up the sleeves and do the work, the payoffs will be enormous; the financial, emotional, and spiritual awards beyond generous.

Here is what's possible.

Tomorrow's great organizations will be known as much for their employer brand as they are for their customer brand. In fact, consumers will be attracted to and identify with the qualities of the tribe that is built to serve and support them. We are stepping into an era in which a yearning for greater focus on human values is increasing. As artificial intelligence and robotics take over rote and monotonous work, the qualities of wakefulness, connectedness, interest, empathy, enthusiasm, curiosity, creativity, responsiveness, and accountability will not only become the central desire of the consumer, but are the same qualities that make an organization that promotes them a great place to work and build a career.

The healthy workplace will be filled with people who've come to terms with ever-increasing change. In organizations that have built "the solution," we will find talent attracted by the quality and brand of the organization's mentors. Want to grow a career? Find the mentors who will teach you the skills, give you the role-modeling, and connect you to transforming professional opportunities. It is the quality of your mentors that will determine how quickly you rise or develop comfort and confidence. This is how the world always worked; it was simply obscured in the obtuse workplace left over from the Industrial Revolution.

Mentors have always been the early adopters of success. They have always been the most prized sources of help. We institutionalized cubicles. Why not institutionalize compassion? The organization's mentors will be the adopters of cultural characteristics and standards of excellence, as well as purveyors of change and engagement. Mentors will be the new elite within the workplace, far more valued than attaining a particular caste on the organizational chart. Of course we will continue valuing what someone did, but we accomplish so much more when we help someone grow into a new and more vital contributor. It is the mentors who take responsibility in helping others become better, stronger, more capable, and more successful. They take newcomers under their wing, and they live for those meaningful moments of uplifting others.

In this new workplace, we don't encourage our people to learn the skills of communications, sales, presentations, and relationship-building simply to connect with our customers. We teach them so they connect with life and everyone around them. We teach them to present because in so doing, they take ownership of their work. We teach them to sell so they start asking great questions and listen more appreciatively to others. They become keenly aware and skilled in finding others' needs and expectations. Most of all, we teach them these skills so they can end the dreadful isolation that is sweeping so much of our talent to the sidelines.

In taking this initiative on, we also can require and expect so much more from ourselves and one another. For those who refuse to listen or respond, we don't have to wait years before their obsolescence becomes blatantly apparent. We build cultures that attract the souls that stand in the open, appreciate being seen and seeing others, and view transparency as the means to stay on top of the waves and thrive. In building tomorrow's engaged worker, there will be nothing to hide. Talent will no longer be gripped by fear. Flying below the radar will only happen in organizations that also fly below the radar and eventually disappear without a trace.

The mentor-driven, growth-driven culture of tomorrow will not be taken very seriously. If you mean it, you will find someone who is succeeding in every area you want and need to succeed in. What you don't do is hang out with other workers who are infected with negativity or disengagement. For example, if you want to become a rock star in technology, you find a mentor who is a rock star in technology and you do whatever it takes to carry that person's water. You follow their instructions. You listen. You study. You are humble and respectful. If not, you are shown the door.

When an egregious customer service incident happens, it will not fly to blame it on the union. As labor laws have developed the sophistication to protect the worker, unions will have to become skilled partners with employers in helping workers embrace active learning, hitting performance standards, and staying competitive with the changing workplace. Absent that, unions will become progressively more outmoded in trying to hold off change through detrimental behavior. It will not be acceptable to blame a lack of training on workers, because engaged workplaces will be filled with individuals who always learning and thus strong in life skills. Other organizations will have to pay more to attract talent in the absence of a great culture, but the best of the best will still not want to work there—or stay there.

Hiring managers will make more skilled hiring and promotion decisions. They also will be aware of their own bias and often will hire more of the people who used to give them pushback. Here's why. If a candidate has the kind of strong human skills, ethics, and values that will make them a great worker and the organization has a strong mentoring program, why *not* select that person? In fact, how many more awards, technological breakthroughs, sales, retained customers and other advancements will come out of mentors turning the very workers we might have dismissed into stars? It is mind boggling to think this one through. This is one of the many reasons I propose making mentorship a fiercely important aspect of your culture.

Where does this narrative leave the CEO? Let's begin by examining the job's promise.

The title, CEO, implies mastery. As human and organizational evolution accelerates, however, CEOs will be left with no alternative but to demonstrate mastery by continuously developing their own culture. Boards and investors are wising up. They are realizing the connection with the market and profits is determined by the strength of the connection we have with our people. The kind of lazy, cynical, and even contemptuous attitude towards employees is showing up in the bottom line with ferocity. And, as financial and performance oversight becomes more educated about the ways of engagement, expectations will raise around the fact that even an average CEO can lead an awakened, responsive, enthusiastic band of brand ambassadors.

For organizations that dive into *The Workplace Engagement Solution*, the days of getting rid of employees because they cannot keep up with change will no longer be the routine. Of course, market fluctuations will continue to impact the workforce, and performance challenges will come up. But, the needless loss of institutional knowledge, valued relationships, and cultural depth will be the things that get shown the door. The people who work for us and with us not only learn how to change, but they also will know it is expected, nurtured, rewarded, and required. Our colleagues come with us—sometimes confronted, sometimes inspired, sometimes even dragged—but they will be pulled forward as valued members of the tribe.

Insisting that our cultures become filled with active learners ensures a competitive edge that eludes most organizations today. It also creates environments in which talent is constantly evolving, adapting, growing, and becoming. How exciting! *Becoming*. No longer waiting, no longer holding on, but learning and becoming.

As the chief human resources officer continues to evolve into a chief talent officer, we will find professionals who work as partners with the business owner or CEO in developing awake, alive, and fully engaged organizations. The talent officer wouldn't consider taking over the culture. In fact, if a CEO asks someone else to do the job, that person ought to dust off their resume and leave. The fully engaged CEO looks for a savvy, emotionally aware professional to lead the business of people and become an advisor on how to build human capital, grow overall intelligence, produce loyalty, inspire collective courage, make change an attractive adventure, and always protect transparency.

People will not join your organization because they want to set themselves in park and grow old there. People will join your organization because it is the best place to grow. People will join your organization because they can be their absolute best with you.

Consider the alternative: How many of our nation's consumers have lowered their expectations and think of calling a service provider with dread? How many of us stand in line with a cashier who doesn't want to be there? How many workers, parents, and families live in a trance because we literally dull their lives for eight hours a day? How many of our valued citizens have fallen into the scourge of under-employment because we didn't show them how to come along on the journey of change? If we allow this departure to continue, how much will we have to pay in order to take care of them? How many of us are picking up after employees because we didn't take the initiative to change ourselves?

In the 1980s, I worked with an organization that helped more than 80,000 gays and lesbians come out of the closest. Years later, I was asked what that experience contributed to my work today. I responded, "Everyone who comes into one of our programs is in the closet about something!" They are hiding a dream or aspiration, or they have a precious gift and are afraid of the attention if it comes into the light. Some of them are quietly desperate and unhappy because they are barely meeting the needs of their families. Some have disliked who they work for and observe that nothing changes because it is never voiced. Some have grown bitter because they have always been better than the job at hand but never learned how to get anyone to notice. Yes, in our programs, I have watched thousands of souls step forward and express who they really are, what they are capable of, what they aspire to become, and what they need to learn in order to become their best future selves. The coming out process is the same. There is often the fear of survival and the idea that no one will help them. And then, there is light.

Retooling our talent and our culture will take vision and, above all, courage. Changing ourselves will require the best of our humanity, our humility, and our resourcefulness. Developing cultures that actively build the engaged workforce will exude courageous action on both good and bad days, in wonderful and in terrible markets. We will be required to demonstrate a level of vision that rises far above the quarterly spreadsheet and plans for several years ahead.

So, let me propose that if you have extended the honor and expense of hiring someone into your tribe, that investing in that person's greatness will only increase the innate value of that decision, that building a mentor-driven, high-standard, radically compassionate, connected, and open culture will also lead to less house-cleaning and more exciting opportunities.

Can such organizations save lives? Absolutely.

Will such organizations become category leaders? Of course they will.

Actually, they will accomplish far more. We will build new economies. We will build a future devoid of patronizing promises to the past and filled with a courageous vision of what we have earned through our hard work.

The "trance" simply must end.

Many have asked me if *The Workplace Engagement Solution* is written for CEOs or human resource professionals or people who want to become more engaged.

Actually, I have written it for anyone who will listen.

APPENDIX

Question Library

The deep value and benefits of Socratic inquiry are vast. In the workplace, asking and answering a few key questions can bring a fluid discipline to the day that is far more effective than reviewing a checklist. In fact, consider the reality that if someone is focused only on going over a checklist, this is a ritual that is actually supporting and sustaining disengagement. Many believe that if they focus on the tasks on the list, that they are doing the right thing to align people and outcomes. But this is only partially true.

Alternatively, when we pose compelling questions to the mind, it immediately becomes more active and engaged. When beginning a meeting, for example, asking the participants to answer a few questions related to the topic helps each person take greater ownership of the topic at hand rather than being less participative or totally passive listeners.

The Question Library offered here is an introduction to the Socratic inquiry process. Many of our clients have developed in-house libraries covering all of these areas. You can also invite your employees to submit new questions that raise the bar, uncover new information, and initiate new behaviors. In fact, this is an exceptional way to increase and extend the benefits inherent in the overall process.

These libraries should be accessible to all employees, and everyone should be encouraged to engage with them as well as contribute new questions for a wide variety of applications. Under these circumstances, it is also valuable to appoint a curator to monitor and organize new submissions to help keep the standards of the library high. Alternatively, the process could take a Wikipedia approach, in which new visitors make improvements, once again, through a curator.

When asking questions that can elicit uncomfortable feedback, it is critical to establish certain guidelines. Once you have them, make sure to publish the required behaviors throughout the organization. This will save needless friction. Here are a few pointers:

1.   If you are the individual asking the question, simply listen or ask clarifying questions. Don't defend, retaliate, react, or dismiss. Make it safe for stakeholders to respond.

2.   If you are the stakeholder answering a question, don't use that moment as an opportunity to shame, insult, or abuse the questioner in any way. Give feedback in ways that are respectful, supportive, and constructive.

3.   Practice taking nothing personally.

4.   Never ever rely on the words "I don't know."

Our first exercise, Irrevocable Happiness, is to be used at the beginning of a Workplace Engagement Solution initiative with everyone. It is also to be used with new hires and for revisiting on a quarterly or biannual basis. It can be used privately, between mentor and mentee, and as an exercise within groups or teams. We encourage frequent reviewing to deepen the definitions and to solidify the pursuit of happiness in your daily awareness. Remember: there is only one incorrect answer, and that is "I don't know."

Irrevocable Happiness

If you were happy all of the time, what would you be doing with your work? How would you be spending your time? Where do you live? How do you feel? Describe your personal and professional lives as if you were "sentenced to happiness."

Career and Change Updates

The following questions can be used by mentors, career counselors, human resources, and talent management professionals. We strongly suggest that everyone uses these questions to stay abreast of the constant need for change.

Active Learning/Skill-Building

1. How do I feel about building my "courage skills"?

2. If I embraced the learning experience, how could these skills impact my future?

3. If I became a master with these new skills, what impact would it have on my life?

4. In moving forward with my career, here or elsewhere, what do I need to learn as soon as possible?

5. Which areas of my job and profession are about to be impacted by change?

6. If I stay, what kinds of new skills do I need?

7. If I move on, what kinds of new skills do I need?

8. What are my biggest fears about the changes impacting my work?

9. How can I take positive action *despite* my fear?

10. Who do I know that could provide insights about the skills I need to be effective with change?

11. How will I learn the skills?

12. How can I make this learning process as pleasurable as possible?

Time Management

These questions are to be used on a daily basis. Modify them as needed to fit the work area and function. We strongly recommend using questions like these at the beginning of each day to develop the ritual as an ongoing practice. These few minutes, in many organizations, represent the most valued time for leveraging productivity. Customize the questions to acknowledge differences in environment, but never remove the spirit of the inquiry.

1. What is the best use of my time today?

2. What is the ideal blend of tactical and strategic activity?

3. Who needs my attention today?

4. How can I best take care of myself?

5. Who deserves my praise?

6. What is the one problem I most want to solve?

7. How can I best market my value, new ideas, and solutions?

8. Where do I need support, improvement, or change?

9. What is my current attitude and how can I improve it?

Mentor Questions

Mentors will be those who have developed a modicum of mastery in questioning others with positive results. They will have committed to the courage skills and learned enough to be objective about their value and use. Through time, mentors can become masters of Socratic questioning because questions are the primary method of connecting people to their truth, opening them up and motivating them to learn, grow, and succeed. Consequently, it is wise for a mentor to keep a journal, add questions to it and explore new ones, and continue to refine the best ones.

Here are a few examples that can get mentors started quickly:

1. What do you want to accomplish in our meeting today?

2. If I become your mentor, what do you want the outcome of mentoring to be?

3. What are some of your challenges?

4. How would you describe your relationships with your colleagues?

5. What do you attribute the quality of your relationships to?

6. Who deserves your praise today?

7. Do you have time management rituals? If so, tell me about them and how they support you in getting more out of your day.

8. Where do you want to grow next and why is it important?

9. What changes would bring you the most joy?

10. What would be frightening, difficult, and worthy for you to pursue?

11. What is the one thing you can do that would make this a transformative year?

Meetings

All too often, those who lead meetings spend little time evaluating how to make the meeting as engaging as possible. Meetings should include inspiring and praising others. It should be so exciting that attendees are motivated to tell others about it. Meetings can be greatly improved by answering a few questions while preparing the agenda and by asking everyone who attends to answer a few questions before you begin.

For the Leader

1. What can I do to make this meeting engaging, interesting, and valuable?

2. How can I best justify the time, manpower, and value of pulling this group of people together?

3. What do I want them to take away from the meeting?

4. What do I want people to tell others about this meeting afterward?

For the Attendees

Always ask the participants to bring paper so that they can write down the questions as well as the answers you will pose to them. There is far more engagement of the whole self and depth of answers in actually writing them out rather than asking them to just verbally reply. Use any questions from this list that are appropriate and add in open-ended questions of your own.

1. How do you feel about (the topic)?

2. What do you want to contribute to (this topic)?

3. How would you describe the ideal outcome?

4. If we need a breakthrough on this issue, what does that look like from your perspective?

5. What kind of help or resources are we going to need to move this forward?

Leadership Development

When we deliver a leadership program at Inspired Work, our questions are customized to fit the business circumstances, current and desired leadership capabilities, and current and desired future state with each significant priority, relationship, and upcoming changes. These are a few question examples for leaders to ask of their people. Customize your own to get the best feedback from your stakeholders. In this case, simply ask the questions and elicit verbal answers. It is important that leaders respond only with more clarifying questions—never answers or opinions—and always thank participants for the feedback.

1. How would you describe my leadership style?

2. What do I do that encourages you to contribute?

3. What do I do that discourages you from contributing?

4. What do you most want to contribute that I could help you with?

5. What do you most want to accomplish at this organization?

6. How can I help you get there more quickly?

7. In your opinion, what does our business unit need that we are not supporting?

8. If you were going to redesign this organization from scratch, what would you change?

9. How can we do a better job for our clients/customers/ stakeholders?

10. How am I perceived?

11. What can I do to improve that perception?

12. In your opinion, what can we do to take advantage of the changes ahead?

Engagement

Engagement is a practice and a way of life. The practice can be undermined by a variety of issues: A colleague becomes distracted and withdraws from the team. Someone becomes more fearful than usual. A team member starts bringing in cynicism or even contempt to meetings and day-to-day conversations. That highly focused partner becomes aimless and lackadaisical.

In the vast majority of cases, gently pointing the symptoms out will open the door to resolving them. In a highly engaged team, temporary circumstances are generally behind these fluctuations in behavior. It is everyone's responsibility to help this individual regain connectedness with the team, the customers, and other stakeholders. If we become resigned and let the disengagement grow, we are sliding back to a disengaged culture.

Mentors, managers, and team members will do well to support the colleague with tact and kindness rather than coming at them with any form of disciplinary process or energy. That is, unless the behavior is egregious.

You want to review and consider all questions before you use them. It pays to really think about what you are doing and why you are doing it. Always strive to be relevant and appropriate. Here are some good sample questions to inquire about engagement. Before and after you begin, be aware of where the individual is with filters such as cynicism, contempt, aimlessness, resignation, and frenzy. Don't use the definitions as a weapon, but rather gently point them out.

1. I have been developing the sense that you are checking out a bit. What is going on with you?

2. How can we help you re-engage?

3. What kind of support do you need to get back on track?

4. If you are overwhelmed with the workload, how can we hit the target without burning you out?

5. You don't seem to be very interested in the skill development process. What will it take to shift your attitude?

6. How can I inspire you to reach out more, present with greater enthusiasm, and ask others for help?

7. I heard about your interaction with the client today. Can you tell me what happened?

8. How do you feel about what happened?

9. If you had a "do over," how would you do it differently?

10. I want to help you succeed. All of us have blind spots. How can I help you avoid this one?

Support Systems

There is almost always a support system to fit any need. Great mentors will confidentially help their clients build new support systems by routinely discussing needs and finding support to fit those needs. We typically look at 15 different areas of a person's life. Rather than providing questions for every single category here, I am providing examples at the beginning and where I feel it may be most helpful. The idea of customized support systems is so alien to many of us that it will be most helpful to define what is meant by each category. It is wise for organizations to start building resources that can provide professional support to everyone. Look for the highest of standards, reputation, and track record of performance.

Following are some key support categories.

Career Development (Short-Term)

These are the career issues that are immediate and perhaps even pressing. They can involve skill-building, starting a big project, transitioning out into a new career, and preparing for a promotion.

1. What do you want to accomplish in the coming year and how can we help you get there?

2. In qualifying for the job that you want, what do you need to learn?

3. What do you need from your team to attain that goal?

It is equally important that individuals ask senior stakeholders questions that help them progress with their careers or set higher expectations.

1. This is the income I would like to make. In the coming year, what value can I bring into our department that will justify that income?

2. Please give me the specific targets I need to hit in order to justify a promotion (or new income).

3. How would you advise that I go about reaching my career goals?

Career Development (Long-Term)

Disengaged workers tend to only address career development when they are in a crisis. In other words, they lose their job and look for another one, often just like the job they hated. They only network when they have to, generally during a transition. Long-term career development is about setting aspirations, finding meaning, developing a legacy, and building self-esteem. Here are some questions that can help focus in on this area.

1. What do you want to accomplish with your life?

2. Describe the legacy you want to create here.

3. How would you describe your overall purpose in life?

4. What do you really want to be doing?

5. What do you need to learn in order to fulfill that ambition?

Finances (Personal)

Issues that come up with finances ought to be handled confidentially with a mentor. These can include qualifying for a home loan, credit workouts, managing tax issues, or simply becoming a better manager with money.

The questions around this will come easily. I suggest that mentors and engagement leaders develop resources that can be given to employees. Set the highest of standards. For example, be careful with financial advisors who sell their own products. Personalized advisement rather than faceless bankers is always better. Shop around and select resources based on reputation and day-to-day performance with referrals.

Risk-Taking

The very purpose of a business leader or mentor is to get more out of people than they would be able to do on their own. Mentors ought to always look at valuable and positive ways to get their clients to stretch and take more risks. This can include reaching out to leaders that come up during social networking. It can include inspiring a mentee to make their first presentation. Often, it includes developing new behaviors. Additionally, as an individual learns the courage skills, he or she will become more comfortable with taking risks.

Mentors are at their best when they push their mentees to grow but not push so hard that the person implodes.

Fear Management

Mentors are ideal for providing comfort and guidance when someone is feeling frightened. But in a hard-charging culture, fears will come up all the time. We want all those who are mentored to develop specific people to reach out to when they get frightened. However, avoid reaching out to people who only tell us not to be frightened or who put us down for having fear, or commiserating with people who share the same fear. In other words, when one starving actor says to another, "Oh, I know how hard it is" nothing changes. A good mentor will say, "Yes, I know it is hard but that's because it is worth it. How can you change your approach in order to be more successful?" Here are some sample questions around fear:

1. This year, you have quite a few opportunities that might raise some fear. How are you going to respond?

2. As you go through this significant growth period, who are you going to reach out to for support and help with any fears that arise?

3. It is always good to have a variety of people to reach to when you're frightened. Who are those people for you?

4. Who are the five safest people for you to reach out to when you are feeling frightened?

Image

Like it or not, most people make a decision about buying or hiring in the first few moments. Our overall image is part of that quick decision-making. Image is a very touchy subject for many people, but it is also an area that can make or break success. I strongly suggest having highly vetted resources in this area. Image consultants ought to be pros who can properly assess a person's ideal colors, cut and style of attire, accessories, hair style, and shoes. At Inspired Work, we have a philosophy that if someone wants to become more successful, it is time to have an objective professional evaluate his or her physical presentation.

An example of a question: "You want to grow your income by 50 percent. How can we upgrade your physical presentation to fit the income expectations?" (In other words, if someone wants to move from $75,000 to $150,000, it is wise to look like a $150,000 person).

Healthcare (Chronic)

When someone suffers from chronic pain, persistent excess weight, low energy, and so on, it is a good idea to find additional resources beyond mainstream medicine for support. Some examples include chiropractic, acupuncture, nutrition, and fitness resources.

Healthcare (Critical)

Many consumers of medicine spend little time vetting and qualifying the person who manages their health. This is an area in which research, references, and interviews lead to far better results than blindly accepting a physician.

Administrative

Typically, this category is about keeping our lives and our businesses organized.

Wellness

This is about our well-being. It can include physical fitness, health, energy, and vitality. What are we doing to support these categories? What kind of support do people need?

Happiness

Happiness is the single best indicator that we are doing the right thing, that our life is on the right track, that we love our work, and that we love our lives. Asking questions about happiness is a good idea. Building support systems that ensure our happiness is also good.

1. Have you written out your version of irrevocable happiness?
2. How much energy are you giving towards being happy?

Play and Leisure

This one truly needs no explanation.

1. What do you do for fun?
2. When was the last time you took a vacation?
3. What would be your best next vacation?
4. How often do you laugh?

5. What do you do to get work out of your mind?

6. What is the most fulfilling and wonderful thing you could do with your time off?

Other

All of us have unique and unusual needs that can include finding a dog sitter, a party planner for our parent's anniversary, a spiritual coach—the list is endless. The point is, believe there is a solution to every problem.

• • • • •

And, that is my intention for all of you. I wish for you to lead well-balanced lives, to be happy, to love going to work, to love being part of your tribe, and to love the people that you work with, work for, and who work for you.

Notes

1. The Great Disengagement

1. Annamarie Mann and Jim Harter, "The Worldwide Employee Engagement Crisis," *Gallup Business Journal*, January 7, 2016.

2. *http://joshbersin.com/2015/09/a-new-market-is-born-employee-engagement-feedback-and-culture-apps*.

3. Alvin Toffler, *Future Shock*, (New York: Random House, 1970).

4. Buckminster Fuller, *Critical Path*, (New York: St. Martin's Press, 1982).

5. Jack Copeland, *Colossus: The Secrets of Bletchley Park's Codebreaking Computers*, (Oxford, UK: Oxford Press, 2006).

6. Michael C. Jensen, and William Meckling, "Theory of the First: Managerial Behavior, Agency Costs, and Ownership Structure," (Rochester, N.Y.: University of Rochester, 1976).

2. A Change of Heart

1. *Look Up,* video by Gary Turk, *www.garyturk.com.*

2. Dean Schabner, "Americans Work More Than Anyone," abcnews.go.com, May 1, 2016.

3. Christopher Ingraham, "The Astonishing Human Potential Wasted on Commutes," *Washington Post,* February 25, 2016.

4. Carmine Gallo, "Southwest Airlines Motivates Its Employees With a Purpose Bigger Than a Paycheck," *Forbes,* January 21, 2014.

5. Christopher Elliot, "Southwest Airlines Pilot Holds Plane for Murder Victim's Family," Elliott.org, January 10, 2011.

3. The Art of Change

1. John Wayne, *www.brainyquote.com/quotes/authors/j/john_wayne.html.*

2. "Legendary Duet," *Oprah Show,* May 30, 2008.

3. Seth Godin, *www.brainyquote.com/quotes/quotes/s/sethgodin412226.html.*

4. Geoff Colvin, "How to Build the Perfect Workplace," *Fortune,* March, 2015.

4. Mission, Vision, and Purpose: Fuel for Change

1. Maya Angelou, *www.brainyquote.com/quotes/quotes/m/mayaangelo392897.html.*

2. George Washington Carver, *www.brainyquote.com/quotes/quotes/g/georgewash158551.html.*

3. "Peanut Man," *Time,* June 14, 1937, retrieved August 10, 2008.

4. Starbucks, "Our Mission Statement," *www.starbucks.com/about-us/company-information/mission-statement.*

5. The Visibility Initiative

1. Elie Wiesel, *www.brainyquote.com/quotes/authors/e/elie_wiesel.html*.

2. Dale Carnegie and Joseph Berg, *The Art of Public Speaking*, (North Charleston, S.C.: CreateSpace, November 9, 2015).

3. Gary Vaynerchuk, *www.brainyquote.com/quotes/authors/g/gary_vaynerchuk.html*.

4. Jim Rohn, *www.goodreads.com/quotes/1798-you-are-the-average-of-the-five-people-you-spend*.

5. "The Influencers," *60 Minutes*, CBS News, October 23, 2016.

6. The Support System

1. "62nd Academy Awards." *https://en.wikipedia.org/wiki/62nd_Academy_Award.html*.

2. Oprah Winfrey, *www.brainyquote.com/quotes/quotes/o/oprahwinfr132401.html*.

3. Norman Vincent Peale, *www.brainyquote.com/quotes/quotes/n/normanvinc109427.html*.

4. Bill Walsh, *www.brainyquote.com/quotes/quotes/b/billwalsh405751.html*.

7. What Is an Engagement CEO?

1. Richard Branson, "Virgin America: Look After Your Staff," *www.virgin.com/richard-branson/look-after-your-staff*.

2. Cale Guthrie Weissman, "Why Marissa Mayer's Talent Acquisition Strategy Failed," Fast Company, July 26, 2016.

3. "The Highest Rated CEOs List," Glassdoor, *www.glassdoor.com/Award/Highest-Rated-CEOs-LST_KQ0,18.htm*.

4. Jeff Schmitt, "Executive Q&A Bain's Bob Bechek," Poets & Quants, April 30, 2016.

5. Hope King, "This Tech CEO Is More Loved Than Mark Zuckerberg, CNN Money, June 8, 2016.

6. Laura Entis, "The Top Ten Companies to Work For" *Entrepreneur*, December 10, 2014).

7. Glassdoor review, *www.glassdoor.com/Reviews/Facebook-Reviews-E40772.htm*, May 17, 2014.

8. Mark Zuckerberg, *www.azquotes.com/quote/685738*.

9. Jeff Weiner, "Hope You Find His Advice as Invaluable as I Have," LinkedIn, *www.linkedin.com/pulse/20140210025756-22330283-five-keys-to-happiness*

8. The Right Fit

1. Jane Porter, "You're More Biased Than You Think," Fast Company, October 6, 2014.

2. Ibid.

3. Geoff Colvin, "How to Build the Perfect Workplace," *Fortune*, March 5, 2015.

4. Glenn Rifkin, "Big Data, Predictive Analytics & Hiring," (Korn Ferry Institute, *Briefings*, May 12, 2014).

9. Mid-Management: Engagement's Final Frontier

1. Jack Zenger and Joseph Folkman, "Why Middle Managers Are So Unhappy," *Harvard Business Review*, November 24, 2014.

2. Robert McKinney, Michelle McMahon, and Peter Walsh, "Danger in the Middle: Why MidLevel Managers Aren't Ready to Lead," *Harvard Business Review*, March, 2013.

3. Ethan Mollick, "Why Middle Managers May Be the Most Important People in Your Company," *Knowledge@Wharton*, May 25, 2011.

4. Joe Klass, *The 12 Steps to Happiness*, (Center City, Minn.: Hazelden Publishing, 1982).

Index

About the Author

In 1990, David Harder founded Inspired Work, dedicated to helping individuals transform their relationship to their work. In 1997, David's first book, *The Truth About Work* (Health Communications), was published, delivering insights into how to move beyond simply making a living to building a richly fulfilling professional life. The first several thousand participants in the Inspired Work Program served as case studies in how to have these breakthroughs.

In 2001, Mr. Harder was asked to redesign the Walt Disney Company's leadership program. His groundbreaking process uses existing business challenges as the learning opportunity and provides customized stakeholder inquiries conducted directly by the executives. This immersive learning experience produces highly branded leaders who skillfully connect with the needs and expectations of each stakeholder—a watershed change in fulfilling the needs of modern leadership.

For many years, employers were reluctant to provide Inspired Work's initial and signature program to all employees. The fear was that if every employee connected with the truth and personally changed, most of them would also leave. Quite the opposite happened. In environments like the University of Southern California, intact teams had immediate breakthroughs with employee engagement and the results were sustained. In fact, the benefits only deepened over time. In this environment, it became vividly clear: Full employee engagement hinges on the ability of each team member to change and to help others change. And, it can only succeed as a highly involved, collective, and democratic solution.

Inspired Work has served a wide variety of organizations, including HBO, Sony Pictures Entertainment, Loyola Marymount University, the University of Southern California, the United Church of Religious Science, Morgan Stanley, Smith Barney, Baxter Healthcare, the Art Institute of America, and many others. David Harder's leadership, career development, and team building programs produce some of the world's most outstanding satisfaction numbers in any business: 92.6 percent.

David has appeared on many business and human-interest programs including CNN, CBS, KTLA News, KFWB News, and Business News Network. He studied music at USC and is an accomplished jazz pianist. His public speaking venues include such topics as the Four Real Reasons to be Afraid of Change: Four Successful Responses.

In 2016, Mr. Harder was a keynote speaker at the International Human Resource Summit, Tec-Canada, and Ultimate Software's human resources conferences.

For more than 10 years, David Harder has published a bi-weekly essay about work that directly reaches millions of business leaders and other contacts. His articles promote a brand that treats work as a profound opportunity to bring solutions to the world's problems and topics that teach how to become more fulfilled, contributive, and successful. He is a promoter of skilled social networking, and his unique method for building virtual communities is now a curriculum delivered to participants from all walks of life.

David is a syndicated columnist for BizCatalyst360, Execunet, and Recruiter.com.

Examples of David's articles are available at: *www.inspiredworkservices.com/library/blog/.*

Prior to launching Inspired Work, David was a general manager for one of Los Angeles's leading staffing companies and a well-respected jazz pianist/composer well-known in the club and concert scene. He lives at the beach in Pacific Palisades with his partner and two outspoken Dachshunds.